MANAGING DIFFICULT
CHILDREN
IN SCHOOL

Lyndsey Stone

Basil Blackwell

For Robert, with love

First published 1990

© Lyndsey Stone 1990

Published by Basil Blackwell Ltd
108 Cowley Road
Oxford OX4 1JF
England

British Library Cataloguing in Publication Data
Stone, Lyndsey
    Managing difficult children.
    1. Children. Behavioural disorders
    I. Title
    618,92'89

ISBN 0–631–17339–0

Typeset in Sabon 10/12 pt
by Photo·graphics, Honiton, Devon
Printed in Great Britain

Contents

Introduction

The management of pupils with behaviour problems is causing increasing concern in both day and boarding special schools and in mainstream schools as the number of specialist units increases and as more individual pupils are placed or retained in the normal classroom setting. Much concern has been expressed by the media, professional associations and parent groups about the growth in disturbed and problem behaviour amongst children in general.

The Warnock Report [1978] recognised the continuum of learning difficulties through an assessment of special educational needs, and the 1981 Education Act [Special Education] enabled the provision for children with special needs to be made in mainstream schools rather than in segregated special schools. The Act recognised the fact that not all children with learning difficulties were at that time in special education provision. Children with learning difficulties will therefore be found in all mainstream settings as well as in special schools and units. Although learning difficulties do not necessarily result in behaviour problems, behaviour problems undoubtedly affect the child's ability to get the maximum from learning opportunities on offer. The effect of this often results in the child with learning difficulties displaying an increase in problem behaviour as he struggles to keep up with his peers. This is an area of high anxiety for all those involved in both home and school relationships with the pupils and young adults. It is an area where stress, rejection and fear are key emotions for teachers, pupils and their parents.

Four main issues are leading to an increase in problems in this area:

First, as education, correctly, has taken on responsibility for all children with severe learning difficulties, the schools and local community systems have had to respond to what is still a relatively new challenge in educating pupils with disturbed and disturbing behaviour. Many such children would have lived in hospitals, with attendance at school being determined by how settled their behaviour was.

Second, there are increasing pressures in coping with the more disturbed young adults in a community setting when they are between the ages of fifteen and nineteen, and in some cases up to the age of twenty-one in the London area. This pressure is felt more strongly in the SLD (Severe Learning Difficulties) and MLD (Moderate Learning Difficulties) schools where the demand for extended education is for virtually all young people.

Third, as pressure grows for more integrated placements for young people with different levels of learning difficulty, there is a desperate need for support and advice within the mainstream system, for both specialist support staff and mainstream teachers and assistants. Much can be learnt from both mainstream and special needs teachers on the different ways of working with children in the different settings.

Fourth, there is a perceived increase in problem behaviour in mainstream schools, not only from those youngsters who have learning difficulties initially, but across the education system as a whole. An increase in aggression towards teachers has been fully reported in the press, as has a range of examples of disruption in classrooms by pupils.

This book is not intended as a theoretical background to the area. It is intended to clarify areas of problem behaviours, provide down-to-earth advice on how to cope with a range of different situations and open discussion on issues such as the effects of school, home and classroom management on the behaviour of children. It will provide a series of tools for teachers, parents and support staff to use in their management of such youngsters in day, residential and home settings and in the local community.

The issues of stress, rejection, fear and anxiety are openly dealt with. Problem behaviours are clearly identified and the implication of such behaviours in different settings are addressed. There are major sections on how to cope with the problems; how to select an appropriate strategy; selection of the appropriate support agency; arrangement of the classroom or home setting; communications and recording.

Throughout the book professionals and parents should value two main themes; the first being that of tolerance and acceptability, the second being that of the role of the expert. Guidance is certainly needed for all those working in this area, most especially on when behaviour should and should not be tolerated as part of a developmental programme. The role of the expert is a vital one in an area of work where, for the pupil or young adult to be appropriately helped, everyone meeting that person during a day should be able to offer a consistent, supportive role confident in the knowledge that they are playing a part in a consistent handling programme. By taking on the role of expert themselves, parents and professionals will develop a wide range of strategies instead of relying on someone else having the answers.

Each chapter will consist of three elements.

1 A brief *introduction* will raise the issues to be explored and the questions to be answered.
2 The main body will deal with *the issues*.
3 A *summary* of each chapter or sub-section will be provided in the form of key points or practical examples.

The book is intended for practising teachers, non-teaching staff, child-care workers, psychologists and parents. It is also intended to provide the foundation for the increased understanding of the difficulties faced by people working and living with such children. It should help schools to work with parents with more confidence.

NOTE   For convenience, 'him', 'his' and 'himself' will be used, but what is said applies equally to both sexes unless stated otherwise.

1
Starting points

Introduction

The practising class teacher will sooner or later meet a child who displays behaviour problems, a child who not only struggles to keep up with the group, but also disrupts the class and teaching situation. The extent to which this behaviour disrupts will vary considerably according to factors such as the nature of the child's special needs, the size of the class, the subject being taught and the type of school, (ie, special or mainstream). Most teachers would say that they have a clear idea of what constitutes disruptive behaviour to them and can clearly identify those children who they see as disruptive. The children identified will not necessarily, however, pose problems for other teachers, nor will they be seen as behaviour problems all the time. The difficulty comes when it is realised that people have different perceptions of what constitutes disruptive behaviour and therefore identify different children for widely varying reasons. Children who have such problems undoubtedly cause a wide range of difficulties for their parents and teachers, have difficulty themselves in learning and often cause disruption to their peers.

This chapter will examine the effects of behaviour problems on others, the experiences of the child in question, the context in which behaviours become problems and the effects of varying tolerance levels in peers and adults. Finally, the chapter will explore the notion of the expert.

1 Effects of problem behaviour

All professionals reach a point of frustration and suffer feelings of inadequacy at one time or another when faced with the apparently intractable problems of a particular child. The acceptance that such feelings come to all of us sooner or later and that there are tried and trusted ways of helping most children will be the central theme running through this book.

Understandably, in the school situation, the problem behaviour will have the most obvious effect on the teacher. It is the teacher who is perceived by others as well as by himself, to be responsible for teaching as well as managing the child. The teacher is therefore the focus of attention of colleagues, senior staff and parents. To admit to having problems may be seen as admitting to failure if the school is not organised on supportive and shared responsibility lines. Clearly, an increase in tension or anxiety as a result of an overly demanding child can be seen in many teachers. This tension is exacerbated by the knowledge that the child posing the problems will be there the next day or the next lesson and that the behaviour problems will not get better on their own.

In some cases, the teacher may see the problem behaviour as coming from 'within the child' and therefore judge the behaviour to be the responsibility of the child. This view leads to the demand for something to be done about the child, rather than to the teacher looking to his own behaviour and the effects of that behaviour on the child. An extension of this view results in under-expectation of the child, such as when the teacher sees the child's behaviour as the result of the parents or the home background. 'What can you expect when he comes from that sort of home?' There is little motivation in this situation for the teacher to try to help the child to overcome his problems because of the belief that, whatever is done, there can be no improvement.

Parents and professionals share many concerns about the effects of undesirable behaviour in children and young people. From an educational point of view, disturbed or undesirable behaviour can seriously disrupt learning. This is not only the case for the child with the behaviour problem, but also for the other children in the group or class and for the child's brothers or sisters. A disproportionate amount of teacher or adult time will be allocated to the child who is disruptive, thereby resulting in an unequal share of attention for the other children. The knock-on affect of this varies from other children copying undesirable behaviours to missing out on valuable lesson time. The more extreme the behaviour, the more effect it will have on the child himself and on the other children in the group.

It is the extreme behaviours that are given the most attention and elicit the most emotional response because they provoke anxiety and fear from the teachers and parents. It is little consolation to the struggling child or to the distraught parent or teacher that someone in another class situation 'down the road' is working in a more extreme situation. The level of the behaviour problem is directly relevant to the school, class or environment in which the child is placed.

Behaviour problems can cause injury to the child, to another child or to an adult. Strategies for the protection of other children are seen as a priority when working with overtly aggressive children. Such strategies can lead to an increase in the physical abuse endured by the adults concerned.

Self-abusive behaviour is frightening and worrying for the onlooker, who may feel inadequate and helpless as the child seriously abuses himself. As a result, a wide range of often unrelated strategies are tried in an attempt to stop the child from damaging himself. Even in the same setting, different people will respond in different ways, resulting in overt criticism over who is responding in the 'right' way and who is causing more of a problem. As anxiety increases, so too does conflict on the relative value of management strategies. Such a response is most often high profile, with teachers, parents and support staff being in danger of over-reacting, reinforcing the unacceptable behaviour and making panic decisions. In desperation, the psychologist may be called in to provide an answer as to why the young person is behaving in such a way; in extreme cases the young person may be suspended from the class or school, pending either an assessment or re-assessment, or a referral for more appropriate educational provision. The 'answer' in such an instance is to move the child on rather than to try to establish appropriate management techniques to support the child in the existing class or school.

A very few children display such extremes of violent and aggressive behaviour that their needs cannot be met in the mainstream or special class situation. Whilst they should not be exaggerated, the management problems posed by these young people cannot be minimised. They cause extreme anxiety amonst children and staff, can cause harm and actual injury, may require enhanced staff ratios and do seriously disrupt lessons. The problems posed by this group of children are not isolated; they are the most extreme end of a continuum of problems posed by young people with learning difficulties.

The problems faced by parents with a disturbed child are clear. In addition to the embarrassment shared by school staff, parents often feel they must accept public criticism for their own behaviour in 'allowing' the child to behave in such a manner. Great sensitivity and understanding must be employed when sharing good ideas with parents, so that the suggestions made can be accepted as possibilities and not as criticism. It is not unusual for parents of a child with behaviour problems to avoid going out or to avoid using public transport with their child. Many parents are embarrassed to ask anyone to look after their child, or have little confidence in anyone else being able to manage; opportunity for free time and space from their child can therefore be limited. Feelings of guilt, frustration and anger are too often experienced when parents struggle to be accepted themselves at the same time as struggling to give their child a normal up-bringing.

Because children who behave in an unusual way arouse fears in other people, it is important for parents and professionals to educate neighbours and the community. For a family that is already under extreme stress in managing the child this is asking a lot, and therefore close working relationships with the school are essential to help teach others by example rather than to talk about the problem in an abstract way.

Parents are inevitably concerned when their child behaves in an unacceptable, disruptive or embarrassing manner. Such concerns are complicated by feelings of frustration and anger when progress is slow or when external criticism is great. Friends and relatives as well as members of the public are often quick to judge and to pass comments on how people are seen to manage their children; such comments often result in deeply entrenched feelings of guilt and inadequacy. This is, of course, highlighted in those parents who choose to send their child to a special school or who request the relief of respite care. The continuing pressure of looking after a severely disturbed child cannot be fully understood until it has been experienced. Those professionals who have had the opportunity to escort children with learning difficulties on a school journey or who have worked in a residential situation will have had some small glimpse of the pressures involved. The major difference, of course, for the residential worker or for the teacher on a school journey is that the end is always in sight. However difficult the situation may seem, the week will soon be over and duty will come to an end when someone else takes over. This is not so for parents.

In the family setting, where the disturbed child demands a disproportionate amount of time from the parents, feelings of isolation and rejection may occur in the other children. Brothers and sisters can have difficulties in learning brought about by their response to the disturbed child in the family. Brothers and sisters tend to be either excluded from family discussions about the problems posed by the disturbed member of the family or be treated as adults and be expected to make 'grown up' contributions to future plans. Both approaches could well exacerbate the difficulties experienced by siblings in coping with the other child. Bizarre and frightening behaviour exhibited by the disturbed child causes not only anxiety and fear for brothers and sisters but also can lead to confusion as to the 'right' way to behave. Inconsistent responses from parents to the behaviour displayed by the disturbed child and to the behaviour displayed by the brother or sister can result in both confusion and feelings of rejection towards the child with special needs.

Behaviours which result in damage to property give cause for concern to parents as well as professionals. Young people who respond by throwing furniture or breaking windows, not only put others at risk, but also destroy the environment. The effects of such behaviour are destructive, expensive and also have a discouraging effect on those who are teaching or caring for the child. The child who eats anything he finds lying around, from flowers to books, to clothing, demands constant supervision for the sake of his health as well as to prevent him from destroying the environment. Similar behaviour can increase conflict with neighbours, as in the case of the child who constantly fiddles with and breaks aerials or wing mirrors on cars.

Professionals and parents alike are concerned not only with helping young people to learn, but also with the right of the individual to live as part of a family and to take his place as part of the community and part of a school, with equal access to a wide-ranging curriculum and as normal an education as possible. Within both mainstream and special schools, young people who display behaviour problems are often segregated and isolated by their behaviour, and so denied equal opportunity for learning. This in turn has an effect on the learning difficulty and often results in a further deterioration in the child's behaviour.

KEY POINTS

- The problem behaviour affects other children, parents, brothers and sisters, the teacher, the senior management team, the head, as well as other professionals.

- Everybody living or working with children experiences children with behaviour problems at some time or another.

- The school has a responsibility to help the community to understand the problems experienced by some children.

- There is a wide range of strategies available for supporting and helping children with learning difficulties and behaviour problems.

Effects of problem behaviour on the child

It can be argued that the first person to experience behaviour difficulties is the child. It is the child who has a realisation that he has failed, that he is struggling with work or with relationships. It is the child who is lonely, always in trouble, continually being punished or told off. That is not to say that he perceives his problems as behaviour difficulties, but that he realises that he is struggling and responds in the only way he knows how, be that aggressively, rudely, by withdrawing or in a range of other ways. It also appears that the child with difficulties is unlikely to realise that some of his problems are caused by lack of appropriate responses on his part; he will certainly, however, be aware that he has not got the skills necessary to cope with the situation and will often become increasingly frustrated and in turn disturbed.

Robert

Robert was an eleven year-old boy who attended a school for children with moderate learning difficulties (MLD). He spent much of his time outside the classroom or out in the playground. It was impossible to catch him if he did not want to come into class. Robert ran from one classroom window to the next, teasing and shouting at the children who were trying to work. If anyone told him to come in he would respond abusively, normally personalising the abuse in order to cause the most offence. Contact with his parents was minimal and he believed that they did not want him or care about him. He rarely showed any pleasure in positive achievements and always seemed to be involved if there was any trouble. If not the instigator, he would be on the periphery. Staff had numerous examples of Robert's unacceptable behaviour and consequently assumed that, if there was any trouble, it would be his fault.

As a result, Robert said, and behaved as though, he did not care. He continually said that he would be blamed anyway, and no one could do anything about him because they were not allowed to by law. Robert had managed over a long period of time to isolate himself from positive relationships with adults or other children.

It is interesting to note that many children who bully others and dominate in the playground have not learnt more appropriate ways of making friends and relationships. They are likely to be unhappy children, isolated from their peers and usually unpopular with adults. The behaviour can be seen to be so unpleasant that it may be difficult to see beyond it to the child who clearly has major problems.

Most behaviour problems accentuate the differences between the child and other children. Bizarre body movements and strange outbursts reinforce the view that the child is different, 'not normal', and often results in fearful, intolerant and cautious responses from other people. The behaviours therefore compound isolation for the child and for his family. Obsessional and ritualistic behaviours come into this group, sometimes resulting in aggressive responses from the child when an attempt is made to break into the ritual. This is particularly likely when the child has indulged in a series of obsessional behaviours for a long period of time.

Some behaviours are so unpleasant and anti-social that they seriously damage relationships with the child. Not only do these behaviours cause extreme embarrassment, but they can also result in complete rejection by parents and professionals alike. A child of three who wets his pants in public is acceptable: an adolescent who is doubly incontinent and then smears faeces is likely to provoke feelings of rejection in many people. More extreme behaviours in this category might include spitting, regurgitating, breaking wind or masturbating in public. It can be very difficult to enjoy working with a child who continuously exhibits any of these behaviours. It is also very difficult to encourage other children to accept and be friends with a child who exhibits such behaviours.

A child who is seen to engage in these anti-social behaviours deliberately will have less sympathy than a child with a physical problem which leads to the behaviour, or a child who has no understanding of the effect of his behaviour on others. The first child is likely to have angry and disgusted responses from adults and other children, which lead him to repeat the behaviour to irritate and annoy the adult. The child at this stage does not realise (or says he does not care) that he can alienate some adults permanently. Children quickly realise if adults do not like them, but rarely realise that they may have to take some responsibility for the deterioration in the relationship. A child who has behaved in such a complicated negative manner will probably not have the inter-personal skills to repair the damage done. Indeed, do many adults?

Susan

Susan was eight years old and referred to a school for children with emotional and behavioural disorders (EBD) from her mainstream primary school because of her bullying behaviour and aggressive responses when checked. Susan was in trouble so often with the dinner supervisors as well as with her class teacher that she was falling behind in her work. She was therefore getting into trouble at home because she was not making the progress her parents expected. Staff were experiencing serious difficulty in liking Susan because of the way she behaved with smaller and younger children. Needless to say, Susan knew that people did not like her and when her mother threatened that, if her behaviour did not improve, she would have to go to another school, Susan became more disruptive and aggressive to others.

It is often difficult for the adult to stand back and try to sort out what is happening when faced with a child who is being extremely rude, defiant or non-compliant. The natural reaction is to try to stop the behaviour and to 'make the child behave'. Inevitably, this leads to an adult/child confrontation, possibly with both people getting angry and probably with the child's behaviour deteriorating. It is surprising how often the child believes he has a grievance or a problem that could be sorted out if the adult could only find time to listen. The child will always be the loser in a situation of confronation with an adult, even if at the time it does not seem so.

KEY POINTS

- It is the child himself who experiences the behaviour difficulties, and therefore it is the child who receives the positive and negative reactions from others.

- The more complicated and extreme the behaviours exhibited, the more isolated the child.

- The child has the difficulty in behaving appropriately whilst the adult has the problem of how to help him overcome his difficulties.

3 *Behaviour in context*

Many children, of course, behave in different ways in different settings, and it is well known that some pupils are disruptive only with certain adults. Everyone can quote examples of trying, unsuccessfully, to coax a non-compliant child to follow a request, using every method possible, only to have another adult come along and ask the child to do the same thing with a positive result. The frustrations in such a situation are hard to bear until it is realised that sooner or later it will happen to everyone.

Some behaviours might be manageable in the home setting or the classroom, but they could pose more problems if they occurred in public. This is because people who are used to dealing with such problems are often able to predict their likely occurrence and therefore avoid them. In addition, an enclosed space or an environment designed to minimise the effects of problem behaviour will also minimise the potential risk or danger. For example, the child who runs aimlessly can be contained in the classroom if the furniture is used to restrict his running; should he be in a supermarket, however, he might not only cause a great deal of destruction, but also run the risk of running out into the road and under a car.

Often a child who displays this kind of behaviour has great difficulty in tolerating being stopped by someone else, since the behaviour becomes obsessional and the child needs to complete the ritual. Such behaviours can put the child at risk if he is allowed to continue; on the other hand, there can be a risk to the untrained adult if he tries to stop the child.

Sensitive and consistent management is crucial in preventing danger when managing this sort of behaviour and therefore the child is likely to be coped with more easily and safely in the controlled setting of the home or school.

Stuart

Stuart was a sixteen year-old boy who had severe learning difficulties (SLD) and who looked normal. He had a wide range of language which he seemed to use in context. Unfortunately for Stuart, his language was idiosyncratic and highly repetitive. He also swore in a personalised fashion and accompanied this by laughter, seemingly directed at the other person. He had little understanding of the consequences of his actions and did not understand that people were insulted, angered or upset by his behaviour. Stuart came from a home with little support or supervision and, as a result, was often allowed to roam the streets in London. On one occasion he shouted and swore at a group of young men, who beat him up. His arm was broken in three places. The police knew Stuart well and often picked him up to take him home. He was still allowed to do much as he liked. In school Stuart constantly asked for attention, became highly distressed and physically aggressive if he was stopped from doing what he wanted. He was supervised very closely for his own and for everyone else's safety. There were therefore few serious incidents with Stuart in school.

The way the child looks can affect the responses that child receives from others; for example, the child with Down's syndrome can, in most cases, be recognised as a child with Down's syndrome. Exceptions are made for bizarre and unusual behaviour. A child who has brain damage may not appear obviously to have special educational needs. Should that child display behaviour problems, the general public will not be so tolerant, as he may look 'normal'. Some parents have told how members of the public have told them that 'all the child needs is a good smack' to teach him how to behave. Such criticism increases the pressure of having to manage the child, especially when the parent feels it necessary to explain that the child has special needs.

These extra anxieties and difficulties faced by parents highlight the importance of all children with special needs going out and being part of the community from an early age so that they can be seen, accepted and understood. This is particularly important for children with behaviour problems, so that friends, neighbours and family can learn from an early stage how to behave with them. Other children should be encouraged to play with them and should be told why and how they need extra help to join in.

Clearly, a child with a statement of special educational needs with defined behaviour and adjustment difficulties in a school for children with emotional and behavioural difficulties may well have more extreme behaviours than a child with a statement who is placed in a class of thirty mainstream children. For the teacher in the mainstream class, however, the problems posed by the 'less disturbed' child could well cause as much anxiety and concern.

The expectations of adults will vary considerably in relation to standards of appropriate behaviour. For instance, the teacher in a mainstream secondary classroom may normally expect all the children to sit on their chairs throughout a lesson, whereas a teacher in an infant classroom would positively encourage the children to move around the classroom, exploring the environment. Two teachers working with children the same age may well have different expectations of basic behaviour, according to the style of teaching being employed, the organisation and approach adopted by the school, as well as the subject being taught. The child who talks continuously when he is supposed to be working quietly, or the child who is constantly flicking a pencil or rubber band can disrupt a class of settled, hard-working children. Such problems are likely to be seen as minor in a group of children where some are being encouraged to communicate verbally and others are being taught to sit and attend to a task for a few moments. The child flicking the rubber band could cause more disruption in his class setting than the child who only manages to concentrate for very short periods of time.

Experience plays a great part in determining expectation levels; that is, not the length of experience but the learning that has resulted from experience. The teacher who looks critically at his own behaviour and the setting in which the behaviour problem occurs is more likely to avoid potential problems or dangerous situations by altering the environment in some way. By changing the setting the behaviour may become less dangerous, either to the child himself or to others. The setting in which the behaviour occurs will affect the ability of the responsible adults to manage.

Leigh

Leigh was a ten year-old boy with severe learning difficulties. He had some mobility problems but managed to get around quite quickly when he wanted to. He was referred to boarding school because he had a history of escaping from the family home, usually at night. He managed to find his way to the local police station and was returned after a phone call to his mother and a mug of hot chocolate. Understandably, the chocolate, the attention and the ride in the police car made the whole trip worth while. The situation became untenable, however, when Leigh started to take his three year-old sister out on his nocturnal trips. The parents described the home like Fort Knox at night and yet Leigh still managed to find a key to the door or another way out of the house. Leigh's parents were very concerned that the supervision at night should be tight and were unable to offer safe supervision themselves in the home. The boarding school was able to offer waking night supervision for Leigh. He managed to escape on one occasion, however, but the police had previously been warned and kept him in the police station until he was collected. There was no mug of chocolate and no ride back in the police car – only the long walk back to school.

The pressure upon mainstream teachers to achieve measurable results are considerable, and likely to become more so as the effects of the Education Reform Act and the demands of the National Curriculum are felt. The demand for published results of attainment tests will increase the pressure on teachers to complete schemes of work and programmes of study with their pupils. Children with learning difficulties and additional behaviour problems in the mainstream classroom are likely to lead to an increase in pressures on the teacher at a time when performance of the teacher is under scrutiny. The mainstream classroom could well experience an increase in unacceptable behaviours from children who have problems already because of stricter routines and higher demands on work rate. It is easy to see a situation developing where the teacher, who is expected to show a percentage of children reaching a particular attainment target, lacks time and, indeed, experience to meet the special needs of children with learning difficulties. The mainstream setting is not always geared to support the class teacher in effectively teaching children who fall outside the 'normal' range, either in terms of learning needs or behavioural needs. In-service training and support in balancing the demands for mixed ability teaching within National Curriculum expectations are essential for mainstream teachers.

The severity of the behaviour problem depends to an extent on the perception of the person living or working with the child; the experience of the adult will influence his ability to meet the needs of the child and to cope with the problems as they arise. The teacher's interpretation of his role will also affect the perception of the seriousness of the behaviour problem. If the teacher sees his role in terms of helping students to gain examination passes, then less attention may be paid to ensuring that the less able are making progress. The segregated special school aims to focus on the individual needs of the students rather than on the expectation that all pupils will necessarily complete set syllabuses. The two settings may place different emphasis on the style of teaching and on the expectations of pupils.

Whilst the differing expectations of pupils are not necessarily a positive thing in terms of student progress, the opportunity to teach in a flexible manner clearly supports the child who struggles with learning in a more traditional teaching pattern. The setting in this instance has a very real influence on the range and intensity of the behaviour problems displayed. Just as special schools can share knowledge and experience on planning and implementing individual programmes within a whole class situation, so, too, mainstream schools can share detailed and structured schemes of work. As a result, children with learning difficulties in both settings should have more of their needs met.

Extreme and bizarre behaviours in any setting can result in panic and anxiety, even if it is believed that the behaviour could be managed more easily in a different setting. Such anxiety can lead to demands for alternative school placement, both in the hope that the child can be managed more appropriately elsewhere, and in order to remove the pressure and anxiety caused by the experience in the present classroom. Whilst, in a minority of cases, change may be the solution, the answer can usually be found in the setting in which the behaviour problem occurs. Strategies such as information sharing, communication systems with colleagues and parents, as well as clearly defined procedures in case of problems, will all help to minimise stress caused by extreme and bizarre behaviour problems. Changing aspects of the setting could well have more effect than changing to a new setting.

Emma

Emma was a seven year-old girl who attended a mainstream school. She did not like swimming, which happened every Monday morning, and, as a result, Emma refused to catch the bus in the morning and played truant instead. Emma's parents were not very good at informing the school when Emma was unwell and she had frequent days off sick. It was three Mondays before anyone was concerned about Emma's absence. Emma had spent the three days wandering around the area, frightened to go home because she knew she would be in trouble for refusing to come into school. She was at risk of getting lost, being run over or worse. On the third Monday, the school phoned the police for help to find Emma and to inform her parents that she was missing. Parents and staff alike were extremely anxious about Emma's safety and considered her behaviour in this instance to be extreme, because she had placed herself at risk.

The increase in problem behaviours in mainstream classes and the integration of children with learning difficulties and behaviour problems into mainstream schools and classes will undoubtedly result in anxiety and feelings of frustration amongst teaching staff unless strategies for working positively can be shared and systems of support set up. Attention will be given later to the ways of identifying problems early and preventing major confrontation and crisis through avoidance techniques and structuring expectations and the environment.

KEY POINTS

- Children often behave in different ways in different settings.
- The setting affects the perceived seriousness of the behaviour.
- The way the child looks often affects the public's ability to accept his behaviour.
- People in different settings have varying expectations of what is considered appropriate behaviour.
- Teachers in both mainstream and special school settings have a great deal of knowledge and experience to share and exchange in meeting the needs of children with behaviour problems.
- It is often more useful to change aspects of the setting than the placement itself.

4 *Tolerance and tolerance levels*

Tolerance levels vary from individual to individual, from school to school and even, as shown by the Elton Report, from LEA to LEA. Within that variation, individual teachers vary in their ability to cope with a particular problem from one day to the next. So do parents. Changes of mood, differing states of health and factors as simple as tiredness all affect an individual's ability to cope with problems.

From that starting point, it can be seen how complex management of behaviour problems is for the classroom teacher. Even the teacher who appears to agree to implement a series of behavioural strategies one day, may not be capable of doing so the next. Whole-school policies and support networks are indispensable if a teacher is to follow through agreed programmes. Everyone has 'bad days'. The reasons will vary from something perceived as trivial to a major problem causing acute anxiety. It is easy to imagine the conflict and tension between teacher and pupil if both experience a 'bad day' at the same time. The question of tolerance is not, therefore, solely to do with levels; it can also be to do with understanding and with the way an individual feels at a certain moment.

Maurice

Maurice was a ten year-old boy who attended an MLD school. After a period of relative calm and co-operation Maurice's behaviour suddenly deteriorated into non-compliance, rudeness and a return to running away, school refusal and a general attitude of non-caring. The staff felt that he was unable to behave well for long; this reinforced the view that Maurice was badly placed and should be referred to another school for the extra help that he obviously needed. He said he did not care anyway. After this had gone on for a few days he was able to express, in anger, a reason for not caring. He shouted at his teacher, telling her that his mother was in prison and his step-father had told him that, if his behaviour did not improve, he would be back in care. With that knowledge we were able to work with him and his behaviour improved.

Knowing a reason for the behaviour problem helps adults to understand what is happening for the child, so that they can be more tolerant. An understanding of the trigger to the behaviour can lead to the selection of an appropriate management strategy. In this instance, discussion with the step-father enabled him to understand Maurice's confusion and anxiety and so to be more tolerant with Maurice. He also talked about his own worries with him and listened to what Maurice had to say.

This acceptance or tolerance of the needs of others is not always easy, particularly when external demands for results are increased on the teacher. Many teachers will describe their frustration at other children 'losing out' because of the disproportionate amount of time taken up by one child or by a group. Sometimes this frustration turns into anger directed at the child who is misbehaving; at other times it becomes a feeling of failure on the part of the teacher. Either way, it is counter-productive. Clearly, the time taken to meet the needs of the individual through a whole-class or whole-school approach is likely to be less than the time taken to 'deal' with the child posing the problem. The positive use of adults' attention and energy will lead to a decrease in problems and an increase in positive relationships with the child. It is interesting to listen to the balance of staffroom conversation; a few names crop up regularly, some daily. The children who are discussed the most are not those who are achieving the most, or even those who are making reasonable progress, but those who cause the most stress to teachers, the children whose behaviour teachers find the most difficult to tolerate. The discussion is important in order to relieve stress, but should be redirected into a profitable sharing of ideas, otherwise, there is a danger that the discussion will reinforce the negative perception of the child, rather than reveal a deterioration in his behaviour.

Whilst discussing the subject of tolerance and tolerance levels it is useful to include views expressed by children as to why they work for some teachers and not for others. A large number of children with behaviour problems do not want to be in school, and when pushed for reasons will describe teachers picking on them, the work being boring and there not being any point because they 'do not learn anything anyway'.

Pupils show their lack of tolerance for teachers in a variety of ways, ranging from non-attendance to extreme rudeness, to non-compliance and generally disruptive class-based behaviour. Whilst the reasons for problem behaviour cannot and should not always be associated with teacher skill, it is interesting to note a range of pupils' perceptions of good and bad teachers:

Bad teachers

– have favourites
– are not ready for lessons
– are late to lessons
– are rude to children
– don't know the children's names
– don't mark homework
– let some children get away with things and not others
– shout at children
– don't help when the work is too hard
– don't like some children
– waste time
– are too strict
– do not listen to children
– do not give children a second chance
– are friendly out of class but not in class
– leave the classroom half-way through a lesson
– do not care if children work or not
– are moody
– do not bother to mark classwork

Good teachers

- get angry sometimes, when there is a reason
- listen to all sides
- stick to the rules
- treat all the children fairly
- say sorry when they have done something wrong
- give interesting lessons
- always have things for the children to do
- always mark classwork and homework
- ask the children what they think
- are on time for lessons
- stop children behaving badly
- deal with bad behaviour quietly [do not shout]
- are the same every day
- try to make the children understand

Children find disruption in the classroom as difficult to tolerate as teachers do. Clearly, they have strongly held views on what they as pupils expect from good teachers and give some interesting pointers towards what they are expected to tolerate from teachers. Children who cannot be described as having behaviour problems are far more likely to 'play up', resent or dislike the teachers described in the first group. It is little wonder that children who already have learning difficulties or behaviour problems will be unable to tolerate 'bad' teachers.

Children have different tolerance levels at different stages of development. For example, very young children cannot tolerate or cope with long periods of inactivity, they often cannot share or take turns, or concentrate for long periods of time. Equally, the child with a learning difficulty may well have a problem in tolerating failure and as a result behave in an apparently inappropriate manner, for example, tearing his work up. When looking at the question of tolerance levels of adults in relation to difficult behaviour it must never be forgotten that children vary as much in their responses and the reasons for their responses as adults do.

Many problems which would be totally unacceptable elsewhere are, of course, tolerated in special schools or units. There is a real danger in special schools and units of not having on-going or recent experience of what is considered 'usual' and 'normal' behaviour in children. Staff can get out of touch with normal development and normal behaviour patterns for certain ages.

Expecting teachers in a special school to tolerate what would be totally unacceptable in a mainstream school is, to an extent, linked to the view that the behaviour is 'part of the handicap'. The handicap can on some occasions become the excuse for the child's lack of, or slow, progress. Much criticism has been levelled at special schools in recent HMI reports because of the low expectation levels of pupil attainment and progress. It has been suggested that teachers move so far away from normal expectations that children under-achieve. The National Curriculum must be welcomed in this respect, as special schools will need to provide a curriculum in line with what is being taught in mainstream schools. Efforts will need to be made to provide access for each child to as much of the National Curriculum as possible, whatever the learning difficulty or behaviour problem. A balance needs to be struck between tolerance of what is the result of the special need and appropriate expectation of the individual child, so that all children have every chance to contribute as fully as possible to society on leaving school.

The level of disturbed behaviour is only one aspect of the problem in identification and management terms. Not only do children respond in a different manner with different adults, but adults have different tolerance levels for certain forms of behaviour, in terms of what each adult finds irritating, and in terms of accepting a behaviour one day and finding it totally unacceptable the next. For example, continual chattering in class may be ignored one day, but may annoy the teacher so much on the following day that he loses his temper. As far as the child is concerned, he has done nothing different from one day to the next. The changing tolerance level of the teacher has given confusing messages about the child's behaviour. The teacher may be able to cope with the chattering for the rest of the week and therefore is the one behaving in an inconsistent manner. With a more complex series of behaviours, the result can be an increase in the unacceptable behaviour as the child struggles to find out the rules.

Just as two teachers may have different tolerance levels of the child's behaviour, so the home and school may vary in what they find acceptable. The child may be seen to be behaving in an accceptable way at home because the behaviour he is exhibiting does not cause a problem of management to the family. A child who throws food when seated at the table in school may behave quite differently in the home, where he is allowed to walk around eating and is not expected to sit at the table and eat with others. Circumstances and expectations affect how much of a behaviour problem the child is seen to have. A child who swears continually in school, using unacceptable and offensive language in many situations, may have parents who use the same language in the home. For that child, his language is normal and he is not seen to have a problem at home. The inconsistent expectations of home and school result in his behaviour being tolerated in one setting and not in the other. In such a situation it will be difficult to establish a consistent approach between parents and teachers. It must also be accepted that many parents may feel uncomfortable talking to teachers, not only because of anxiety and guilt about their child's behaviour but also because they may have had negative experiences in school themselves. They may be defensive when discussing their child, giving a more positive picture of the child at home than can possibly be true. They may find it easier to tolerate the child's behaviour in the home setting.

Whether the child's behaviour is seen as manageable in the home setting or not, parents have some responsibility for the behaviour of their children in school. That responsibility should be a shared one and should come through close working relationships between parents and school. The Elton Report recommended that the government should explore the possibilities of imposing civil liability on parents for their children's acts in school. The Committee were particularly concerned to make parents legally responsible if their child's behaviour resulted in damage or injury, but this recommendation was not included in the government's response. However, it is widely accepted that schools must take the initiative in establishing and maintaining links with parents, in this as well as in all other areas.

KEY POINTS

- Different levels of behaviour can be tolerated by different individuals.

- Tolerance levels can vary from day to day, from individual to individual, from school to school and from LEA to LEA.

- Children have different tolerance levels in the same way as adults do.

- Children are expected to tolerate good and bad teachers and still behave appropriately.

- Tolerance of unacceptable behaviour is not in the best interests of the child or the adult.

- Whilst tolerance levels between home and school often vary, it is essential to establish close home-school links.

5 *The notion of the expert*

The acceptance that working with children who have behaviour problems is a normal part of the teacher's role is the starting point for looking at the notion of the expert and questioning who should take on that role. The teaching profession, parents and the media have expressed varying concerns about violence and indiscipline in schools, which indicates a level of anxiety in all age groups and at all levels of education. The Elton Committee found insufficient statistical evidence to support the media view that bad behaviour is on the increase and was unable to get a clear picture of the amount and frequency of indiscipline. However, the seven major associations of the teaching profession, which were consulted at the time, reported that their members were concerned about disruptive behaviour and violence towards staff, and that many teachers believed such incidents were more common than they were five or ten years ago. In the absence of clear statistical evidence, the Committee concluded that any measurement of the size of the problem would have to be based on the perception of the teachers at this stage. This reinforces the view that, if teachers see unacceptable behaviour as a problem in their classrooms, then they surely have a problem. The size of the problem is not the important issue; but that there is a problem at all.

If teachers are generally concerned at an increase in behaviour problems amongst their pupils, it is the teachers who will have the job of working with the children presenting the problems. The idea that someone else will solve the problem for the class teacher begs the question, who else is there? Obviously, the class teacher cannot effect all the changes that are needed to manage all behaviour problems in schools, but it is certainly the class teacher who is nearest to the problem of the individual child. The referral of the majority of children to different settings, if it were possible, merely passes the problem on to someone else. Attention must be paid to giving the necessary skills to the classroom teacher and to colleagues within schools, through whole-school policies and school development plans.

This will occur through attention to the need, stressed throughout the Elton Report, for concerted action at classroom, school, community and national levels. Of these four levels, the classroom, incorporating teachers and pupils, is given the priority. This is significant in that it is in the classroom that the effects of adult/child interaction are experienced. And it is first and foremost in the classroom that the skills must be understood and implemented. The school's task is to provide an education appropriate to all the pupils on its roll. Its central purpose is that children should learn. The Head is responsible for organising all the resources in the most efficient manner to ensure that effective teaching and positive learning take place, including the school's system for supporting and monitoring the classroom delivery of that learning experience.

The acceptance that behaviour problems in children with learning difficulties challenge not just the classroom teacher is central to the discussion. Working with parents and other professionals to meet all the needs of the child is of paramount importance. Acceptance that education for the child with behaviour problems goes far beyond classroom activities leads on to the question of who should be involved in the 'education' of the child. Teachers and parents are the key educators. Child-care workers in the hostel or boarding-school situation will have as important a role to play in the day-to-day provision of the education, as will other support staff, such as classroom assistants. It is these people, who are in daily contact with the child, who have, or can learn to have, the necessary skills to become the 'expert'.

All professionals need a range of early identification, prevention and intervention skills, enabling a well prepared and structured approach on a day-to-day basis. Awareness of potential problems and the ability to re-direct behaviours through a flexible, yet structured, teaching approach avoids the reliance on responding merely to crisis. Those same skills, ideas and strategies can be transferred to a variety of environments, such as home and local community, as well as to other classes or schools. Such sharing of good and successful practice by those who have experience of the child avoids the often discouraging search for the experts elsewhere.

The acceptance of the need for support and the ability to ask for that support is a crucial aspect of managing children with behaviour problems. Structures need to be set up in schools, hostels and when working with parents, to enable people to identify their own need for help and to ask for that support before crisis point has been reached. A good school will already have a system for supporting and monitoring staff to ensure not only that the children are receiving a quality education but also that teachers are coping with the demands placed upon them. Supportive appraisal schemes are being used to help teachers develop appropriate classroom management skills. A system of self-appraisal can help teachers to identify areas of need in their own work and the styles of support they require.

Such supportive appraisal schemes are beneficial in early identification of problems and clear target-setting to help the teacher overcome specific difficulties. Although the teaching profession has traditionally resisted the idea of someone else observing teachers teach, there is little doubt of the value of such an approach, if sensitively and consistently applied. Just as children cannot be 'treated' in a separate room, the difficulties of management experienced by teachers cannot be addressed satisfactorily away from the classroom. Head teachers and senior staff have an important role in establishing and implementing sensitive and supportive approaches to appraisal. Opportunity should be provided for teachers to observe as well as to be observed and every chance for joint/paired teaching should be exploited. Ways of establishing appraisal, support and development systems will be explored in chapters 3 and 4 and suggestions will be given for early identification of problems.

KEY POINTS

- The adults most closely associated with the child have or can learn the skills necessary to be the 'expert'.

- Teaching children who have behaviour problems is a normal part of any teacher's role.

- Many teachers believe there is an increase in indiscipline in schools. There is concern over violent attacks by pupils.

- The school and the classroom have the greatest influence on pupil behaviour; therefore, it is the school staff who must address the issues.

- Close working relationships with parents and other professionals are crucial.

- Supportive appraisal schemes are essential in the early identification of problems faced by teachers.

2
The problems

Introduction

In order to plan appropriate management strategies for children with
behaviour problems, it is necessary to define the terms used and to set
the scene. Attention needs to be paid to the effects of other children on
the behaviour of the child in question, and the effects of that peer
pressure both from the positive and negative points of view. This chapter
will explore learning difficulties, behaviour problems, the context in
which behaviour becomes a 'problem', additional behaviour problems,
extreme behaviour problems and the question of when it is necessary
to seek outside help. Examples are given of a wide range of behaviour
problems of actual children. In future chapters, those children will again
be referred to when management strategies are discussed.

1 Behaviour

The use of the word 'behaviour' seems to be associated by most people
with 'bad behaviour'. The word 'behaviour' in the context of this book
is used in the much wider context of behaviourism; that is, it covers
anything that the child does or says. Children display both positive and
negative behaviours which affect their ability to learn effectively and to
function as acceptable social people. Positive behaviour can, of course,
be seen as unacceptable if the setting changes. For example, the child
who talks animatedly with friends can be seen as a nuisance in a
situation where listening quietly is expected; constant chatter throughout
a lesson could be seen as disruptive. Shouting in class would be seen as
unacceptable, but shouting to alert someone of an emergency would be
an appropriate behaviour. Setting affects the perception of the behaviour.
The word behaviour does not have any positive or negative connotations
in itself; it is the adjectives that describe the behaviour which imply its
level of acceptability.

When a behaviour is observed it is rarely seen as a behaviour in its
own right. It is usually interpreted against a background of social

systems and rules. People's expectations of the child and the way he should behave at that time and in that place affect the interpretation of the behaviour that the child is exhibiting. It is, of course, much easier to make judgements about acceptable or non-acceptable behaviour if the behaviour is extreme in any way. For example, the child who absconds from class at any opportunity is likely to be seen as behaving in a more unacceptable manner than the child who is just a few minutes late to every lesson. The first child is behaving in a more extreme manner, although, in some cases, the second child could be more disruptive to others.

Behaviour in the context of this book is any observable action, whether perceived by the onlooker as acceptable or not. All aspects of daily life are made up of a series of behaviours; some simple, some complex. Sleeping, talking, writing, running, cooking, laughing are just a few examples of everyday, observable behaviours. Each is made up of a series of interlocking smaller behaviours, often leading to difficulty in isolating exactly which behaviour is being described.

Observation games and quizzes on the television illustrate clearly how different people notice different aspects of a person's behaviour according to what interests them and what is familiar to them. The police identity parade illustrates the challenge to someone who has watched another person do something, to select the person who was involved in the act. When faced with a group of similar-looking people, the clarity of the original observation often becomes blurred. The skills needed to observe and record behaviour clearly can be learnt and applied in identifying the behaviours that are being concentrated upon.

Generally, with children in the class or home situation, it is difficult to stand back and observe clearly exactly what is going on. It is only too easy to miss a sequence of behaviours that affect what is happening to the child, and therefore to make incorrect or misinformed judgements over what has occurred. It is just as important to develop the ability to stand back and look at the effect our behaviour is having on others; this is especially true if the adult demonstrates by his behaviour that the child is behaving inappropriately. Interestingly, people would rarely describe themselves as behaving inappropriately, 'Bad' or 'problem' behaviour is usually described by another person who cannot tolerate that kind of behaviour.

The word behaviour is used to describe any clearly observable action. In order to understand what another person is talking about in relation to a behaviour, the statement must be clear and must describe the behaviour accurately. For example, 'he is always being aggressive towards his sister' is too general a statement to be clearly understood by everyone who knows him. It is not clearly observable. What does 'always' mean in this context, and what does 'aggressive' mean? Both words are open to interpretation.

A clear description of what he does to his sister might be: 'He pulls his sister's hair when she refuses to do what he tells her.' What does he do? He pulls her hair. When does he do it? When she refuses to do what he tells her. By describing behaviour clearly it is possible to establish a starting point for management of that behaviour. It is possible to agree whether it is acceptable to other people or not, because everyone understands exactly what is happening.

Labels used to describe behaviour in a non-specific way have become known as 'fuzzies'; that is, general, ambiguous and imprecise statements which can often be camouflaged as professional jargon, eg. 'he behaves in a hyperactive manner' and 'his gross motor skills are poor'. It is difficult to gain a clear picture of the child's behaviour from either of these statements. A 'fuzzy' does not need to include unfamiliar words to add confusion; the example used earlier of the boy being 'aggressive' could undoubtedly be described as a fuzzy. Most people would think that they understood the word aggressive; it is only when sharing that perception with others that the difficulty starts. Similarly, verbs such as 'to like', 'to enjoy', 'to understand' are open to interpretation and result in fuzzy or general statements. 'He likes painting' or 'he doesn't like music' refer to an impression made by the reporter rather than an observation of the child's behaviour.

It is difficult to be certain that the statement is true when talking about general or ambiguous impressions. How is it possible to tell if a child likes painting? By asking for clarification about what exactly the child has been doing to show, for example, that he does not like painting, the behaviour is pinned down or isolated in an observable task or piece of behaviour. What does he actually do? 'The boy throws the paint brush when he is expected to paint' tells the observer exactly what the child does, and may later lead to the assumption that he does not like painting. the latter is very much secondary to the first need of identifying the behaviour in order to make a starting point for management.

KEY POINTS

- Behaviour can be described as any observable action.

- Behaviour is not good or bad in itself; it is the perception of the onlooker that assesses how acceptable the behaviour is.

- Behaviour needs to be described clearly to ensure that everyone understands exactly what is being talked about. Subjective impressions are not helpful starting points for working with a child with behaviour problems.

2 *Behaviour problems*

The phrase 'behaviour problems' is used widely in most spheres of education to describe a wide variety of unacceptable behaviours in children and young people.

It tends to be used to cover any behaviour that causes concern to the adult describing what the child is doing or not doing. By the very nature of the term, 'problem behaviour' implies something that people want to get rid of. It has certainly been identified (although as we have seen, not always precisely) as giving cause for concern. In some cases, though, the problem behaviour is something that is not apparent enough, such as withdrawal; that is, the child's lack of contact either verbally or physically gives cause for concern, as in the case of the child who wants to mix with others but does not know how to make friends. The child who, on the surface, appears to be working well but, on closer inspection, rarely asks for help or joins in discussions can be struggling as much as the child who displays overtly unacceptable behaviours.

Peter

Peter always appeared to be doing as he was told. He was twelve years old and attended an MLD school. He rarely interfered with other children's work and seemed to be content to get on with any work that was set. The English teacher first expressed concern that Peter did not contribute to class discussions unless he was asked a direct question. On closer examination, other teachers began to report that Peter copied the work of other children, spent time alone in the playground and did not seem to have any friends. His progress was slow and he behaved as a lonely and unhappy child.

Children who respond with anger, who shout or swear, are much more immediately noticed and labelled as having behaviour problems. Aspects such as the size, strength and age of the child will affect the levels of concern shown, just as the timing and setting of the problem behaviour will affect the tolerance levels of individuals managing the child. The level of tolerance to such behaviours varies widely as does the level of acceptance according to the age of the child and the setting in which the behaviour occurs. Very young children, quickly frustrated by their inability to do everthing they wish to do, display temper tantrums and a destructive response to the nearest toys or books, and so do children with learning difficulties. Such responses are, of course, far more unacceptable in a twelve or fourteen year-old who is regarded as 'old enough to know better'.

The four year-old who throws himself to the floor, kicking out and screaming because he does not want to do something, might be seen as usual for a child of that age; indeed, he may well rouse feelings of understanding or empathy in members of the public [or, at least, his parents may]. A fifteen year-old displaying the same behaviour would pose a far greater management problem, would attract a great deal of attention, mostly negative, perhaps some ridicule, and, more than likely, some fear, because he was behaving in a totally unacceptable way for a teenager. Interestingly, such behaviour might be tolerated in a special school where allowances are made; it would not of course be tolerated in a supermarket, even by the members of staff who may deal with the young person in the school setting.

Stuart

Stuart was a fifteen year-old boy in an SLD school. Amongst other problems he had a history of self-mutilation and so had open sores on his face and neck. Understandably, his parents and staff were extremely concerned about the damage he inflicted upon himself and as a result, were relieved when he chose to carry round a piece of blanket as a comforter, which calmed him enough to stop him scratching and picking at himself. This blanket made Stuart look quite strange because it is most unusual for a fifteen year-old to behave in a way that is more normally seen in a very young child. His blanket was accepted in the special school setting but was viewed with concern by members of the public when he was out.

Everyone has experience of children who do not behave. The word 'naughty' immediately springs to mind, encouraging emotional responses. The word 'naughty' seems to imply that the child can control himself but chooses not to; indeed, the amount of control the child is seen to have over his own behaviour often influences the way adults behave in response. For example, the child who is constantly rude or responds in a negative way when asked to do something is most likely to be treated as naughty and seen as behaving in a deliberately difficult fashion. Unacceptable behaviour can be reinforced by the belief that the child has the control, when often he does not have the language, comprehension or confidence to explain what the problem is. With more able children, confrontations can occur as a result of misunderstandings on the part of the adult because there has not been time or an attempt to ask why the child is refusing. The child is then perceived as having the problem, and is labelled as being deliberately rude or difficult.

Christopher

Christopher was twelve years old and had been admitted to an MLD school because he was refusing to work, being constantly rude to adults and consequently not making any academic progress in a mainstream setting. Christopher showed the same patterns of behaviour for the first few weeks in his new school until attention was changed from the tasks he refused to do, to the requests that the teachers made and the way they were phrased. It quickly became apparent that he was extremely embarrassed by his lack of ability in academic subjects and had learnt to refuse to comply before he failed. When requests were phrased in a non-dominant fashion and related to activities he was able to manage he began to join in with the other pupils.

Whilst children with learning difficulties can be and often are naughty, there are many examples of children who are deeply unhappy, withdrawn or troubled and therefore do not respond as the teacher expects, as in the case of Peter (p. 25). Add to that a child who is disruptive, argumentative, abusive, defiant, cheeky, constantly talking, fiddling, lying or bullying and the question of maintaining classroom control becomes a real issue.

KEY POINTS

- Problem behaviour is any behaviour that causes the adult concern because of what the child is doing or not doing.
- Problem behaviours can cover a wide range of behaviours which affect different people at different times.
- Perceptions of behaviour problems will vary according to the age of the child, his size and tolerance of his obvious special needs.

3 *Learning difficulties*

The majority of children who have a statement of special needs are in need of extra suppport. The assessment clearly states the areas in which the child is struggling and puts forward recommendations to meet those needs. Often, they will relate to difficulties in areas such as reading, writing, mathematics, visual and verbal comprehension, and most will include concerns over emotional and social development, ability to keep up with peers and relationships with children and adults.

The Warnock Report (1978) focused for the first time on the 'special needs' of children, stressing the educational needs rather than the unhelpful categorisation of 'handicaps'. The idea of special needs begins to encourage the notion of a continuum of needs instead of the handicapped and non-handicapped stances which lead to segregation. Traditionally, the handicapped child required 'special' education and the non-handicapped child 'normal' education. It is now recognised that most children have some special needs in terms of their learning ability, and that at some time during their school life many children will require extra help and support to learn.

The simplistic suggestion that some children do not learn because they function at a low ability level resulted in the pre-1971 division of ineducable, educationally subnormal and normal children. Children at that time were not only segregated from the mainstream education system, but some of them from the education system as a whole. Instead, they were offered training in junior training centres, received total hospital care or remained at home. The educationally subnormal children were catered for within the education system but in segregated schools, as they were considered to lack the innate ability to learn well. Learning difficulties were not at this stage commonly recognised as part of a continuum of learning needs.

The law changed in 1971 to encompass all children in the education system by right. At the same time, there was a growing realisation that the IQ test did not give a clear indication of the child's educational difficulties. Moreover, the categorisations of IQs-below 50 meaning that a child was severely educationally subnormal [ESN(s)]; from 50 to 70 that a child was mildly educationally subnormal [ESN(m)]; and above 70 of normal intelligence – were increasingly seen to lack relevance. The notion of three distinct groups of children was refuted as professionals gained more knowledge of how children learn and, in parallel, how children fail.

As these artificial barriers were broken down there was a growing acceptance of the notion that there is a continuum of both ability and disability. Emphasis has moved away from the child as the main component of educational success or failure and on to the school, the class and most importantly the teacher and teaching style. Once it is accepted that all children can learn, it becomes a teacher's fundamental responsibility to enable each child to learn. The move away from traditional handicap labels recognises the importance of identifying learning needs and therefore clarifying the style of educational help that is needed for the child to achieve. This process emphasises the positive as well as the negative, the abilities as well as the disabilities. It does not rely solely on studying the child: it also evaluates the system, to ensure that the education on offer meets the identified needs of the children.

KEY POINTS

- Children with a learning difficulty are those who have a greater difficulty in learning than the majority of children of their age.
- The learning difficulty may call for some special provision to be made, whether in a mainstream, unit or segregated special provision.
- There is a continuum of learning abilities and disabilities.

4 Which comes first, the behaviour problem or the learning difficulty?

The children who cause the most concern to teachers in both special and mainstream classes are those who do not learn and those who do not behave. Both groups of children can be described as having learning difficulties because they are not making the sort of progress expected for the majority at that age range. The question of whether the learning difficulty or the behaviour problem came first is of interest in order to clarify the interrelation between the two and so to establish a means of working productively with the child.

Clearly, a child with behaviour problems is likely to have difficulty in learning effectively. Conversely, a child who has learning difficulties is, more than likely, going to present some behaviour problems, particularly if he is unable to keep up with lessons, feels a failure, does not understand requests or is expected to fail. What starts as a learning problem can quickly escalate into negative interactions and an increase in inappropriate behaviour. Inappropriate behaviour resulting from inappropriate teaching is well known, often resulting in a downward spiral, deteriorating rapidly as the teacher becomes more annoyed or anxious and the child becomes more out of control. When a teacher is struggling to manage a class of children who are not coping with the work set or who are unstimulated or bored, the situation rapidly becomes untenable for learning to take place.

Just as one child is often seen as the most disturbed in a class, so one class may at times be perceived by staff as the most difficult to teach in the school. Teachers have been known to describe experiences with particular classes of children with a mixture of irritation and dread, graphically detailing the range of behaviour problems the children have.

Teacher expectations

The difficulty of determining whether the behaviour problem or the learning difficulty comes first in this instance becomes irrelevant, except when it is accepted that, if a teacher expects the class to misbehave, there is every likelihood that it will. As a result, the children will not be able to work effectively, and will quickly drop behind with their work. The effects on the class as a whole and on individuals within the class will remain a cause for concern.

Senior 3

Senior 3 was a class of children in a mainstream secondary school that was known in the staffroom as being difficult to teach. There were two children who had particularly disturbed behaviour in the class, and with most teachers these two managed to incite the class as a whole to a state of non-compliance and disruption. As a result, the standard of work was not high and many children were under-achieving. It took some time to establish amongst the staff that not all the children had behaviour problems, partly because the timetable in the school meant that teachers would come into contact with Senior 3 for only two to six periods a week. Communication between staff did not allow for a clear sharing of concerns and thus most teachers struggled on alone. There was an expectation that the children had problems in learning and that they behaved inappropriately; on most occasions, therefore, they did.

The challenge of teaching a mixed-ability group of children is likely to put increased demands on the teacher's patience and tolerance. The choice of materials is as important as the appropriate pitching of work in order to include all children in an activity. The ease with which the teacher can control and direct the class will depend largely on the involvement and motivation of the children. Children who are struggling to keep up will quickly become frustrated and resort to inappropriate behaviour patterns.

All adults can remember the 'good' teachers at school; equally, the teachers who were not considered good cannot be forgotten, particularly because the subjects that they taught are often the ones associated with boredom and sometimes failure. Children who have problems with learning can quickly reach a stage where not just the subject but also the school can be seen in a negative way. Undoubtedly success breeds success and, similarly, failure is likely to reinforce feelings of inadequacy and lead to increased frustration and failure.

Kenneth

Kenneth was a twelve year-old boy who attended an MLD school. He intensely disliked going to a special school, mainly because he was picked on and teased by other boys out of school who attended the local High. As a result, he believed himself a failure, rarely attempted any work that was set and spent most of his time being disruptive and verbally aggressive. Understandably, the longer this went on, the further behind he became. He was a very angry and, of more concern, he was a very unhappy child.

It would be useful for teachers to look at themselves when trying to work out why the children are misbehaving. All too often the children are blamed for behaving badly, for 'having no manners', for 'not wanting to learn', when the lesson or the teacher is boring, so that the children are likely to be inattentive and 'naughty'. Add to that the difficulties encountered by the teacher who is ill-prepared and uncertain of the direction of the lesson, or the teacher who presents work in either too juvenile or too complicated a manner and some reasons for children behaving in a troublesome way become only too apparent. This is further complicated by the problems faced when children find the work set too difficult and therefore quickly stop trying, reverting to what is seen as disruptive behaviour.

The interesting, well-organised and empathetic teacher is more likely to stimulate and motivate children, solve problems quickly and fairly and meet the needs of the children in the class. This is more easily said than done, but a wide range of strategies for identifying and meeting individual and group needs of children with both learning difficulties and behaviour problems are available and will be described in detail later in the book.

If it is accepted that behaviour problems and learning difficulties inevitably go hand in hand, all teachers will sooner or later have to address the challenge of selecting strategies that will support the children. The unacceptable behaviours and performance levels can be seen as the problem that the teacher has to solve. The child's achieving expected behavioural and work targets depends on the ability of the teacher and the school to suppport the child and on the child's ability to respond to that support.

KEY POINTS

• Behaviour problems can cause learning difficulties and learning difficulties can cause behaviour problems.

- Success breeds success; failure leads to frustration and, more often than not, more failure.
- The expectation that a child or class is going to behave in a difficult manner will usually result in that expected behaviour.
- All teachers share the responsibility for meeting the needs of children with learning difficulties and behaviour problems.

5 *Behaviour problems in all settings*

If the loose description of a behaviour problem as anything that causes concern to the adult is accepted, then, clearly, behaviour problems will occur in any setting; mainstream, special school, special class, home or in public. It would be wrong to assume that a particular age group is more likely to display problem behaviours than another, or to assume that children at a particular point in the ability range are more likely to have behaviour problems than any other. Although the severity of the behaviour problem relates to an extent to the perception of the person working or living with the child, there will without doubt be a minority of individuals in each age range and in each ability range who will display extremes of disturbed behaviour. Such severe and extreme behaviour problems will be discussed further, later on in the chapter.

It is clear that children with behaviour problems do not appear only in special schools, but the difficulty in establishing a shared definition of behaviour problems results in an inaccurate picture of the total numbers of children involved. Every teacher will have experienced a range of problems through all teaching situations, and it can be accepted that behaviour problems can be found in all age groups, all ability groups and with girls as well as boys.

The problems exhibited by different age groups of children can and do vary in terms of intensity. It has been argued that little children in the nursery or infant class who have behaviour problems are easier to cope with because they can be picked up or held with ease; the fact that very young children have not yet developed skills in waiting turns, sitting still or working independently is not always considered. Sweeping generalisations are not helpful to the nursery teacher or mother of three children under six when they are trying to cope. Young children have not necessarily learnt either the rules or the procedure for doing something and therefore may be behaving in a way that would be unacceptable from an older child. The SLD child has the problem of getting stuck in a series of behaviours that might be associated with very young children.

The approach of the teacher will need to change as children get older and demand changing skills. In mainstream, there is a natural development in the style of support offered by, for example, the infant, the junior and, finally, the secondary teacher. This is made possible by the progression that children go through in terms of classes. Teachers become more specialised and at ease with the age group they teach and learn the skills necessary to support that age band of children. Difficulty comes when children do not behave in the way expected for youngsters of that age. As discussed above, children with learning difficulties may well behave in an immature fashion or may not have learnt the accepted modes of behaviour followed by their peers. The problems faced by these children can become more intense in the special school, which has traditionally been an all-age, small school. Because of relatively low numbers the progression throughout the school has not been so obviously marked and, therefore, attention to changing expectations at different age levels has not always been so apparent. Teachers have specialised in curriculum areas with a whole-school emphasis and not had the opportunity to develop age-related specialisms. It has always been asking a lot of special school teachers to provide a quality service to all age groups of children in all subjects.

With this in mind, it becomes more understandable that some teachers find it difficult to respond positively to the changing demands and expectations of children as they grow older. As children grow in understanding themselves, they become more critical of teachers and the lessons they present. There is often an increase in cheek and non-compliance in a testing sort of way; the 'I won't do it and he can't make me' syndrome. This is particularly true as children grow stronger and bigger. The increase in height and strength gives adolescents with behaviour problems the opportunity to be intimidating.

Although there are fewer girls than boys overall in special schools it would be unwise to suggest that one sex displays more or fewer behaviour problems than the other, nor would it be useful to attempt to draw conclusions from the types of behaviour shown by each sex, but attention should be paid to equal opportunity issues when working with all children with learning difficulties and behaviour problems.

The attention that has been given to discipline problems and unacceptable behaviour in the media has led to the view that behaviour problems are the norm. This is not the case, although as has already been said, all teachers experience behaviour problems in some classes and, from time to time, everyone has a tale to tell of 'that class' or, more usually, 'that child'. The tolerance level of the teacher will have an effect on the seriousness of the problem. Undoubtedly, in every class and in every school there is the child who is seen as the most difficult; ironically, there is always another child to take over when the most difficult child moves up or leaves the school. It is not always easy to remember this when facing the problems of the current difficult child.

It is human nature to forget the difficult times that have gone before, when faced with a seemingly intractable problem.

The comparison of relative levels of difficulty becomes irrelevant when working directly with the child posing the problems or when supporting parents or teachers in their work. To the adult struggling with the child who is suffering emotions of guilt, inadequacy and anger there is little consolation in the knowledge that someone else is working with a harder problem, with more stress or less support.

Problems of behaviour are subject to a wide variety of responses from people the child comes in contact with, and the child is therefore constantly challenging expectations. Adults' responses can increase children's behaviour problems, which is why it is essential to recognise that behaviour problems can be experienced in all settings. What starts off as a small problem can increase if not managed effectively. All teachers need to accept the responsibility for meeting the needs of children with behaviour problems just as they must meet the needs of children with learning difficulties.

KEY POINTS

- Behaviour problems will occur in any setting; mainstream, special class, special school, home or in public.

- Behaviour problems can occur in all age groups although the form they take may well alter from one age to another. Adults need to be able to change their response to reflect the differing needs of children as they grow older.

- The differences in problems displayed by boys and girls should not be over-emphasised; it is more important to meet the needs of individuals then to categorise and generalise.

- One child always has the position of being the most difficult in any class or school – there is always another child to take over when he or she leaves.

- All teachers need to recognise and meet the behavioural needs of children just as they have a responsibility to meet the learning needs of children.

6 *Perceptions of behaviour problems*

The way that the behaviour problem is perceived by the adult will affect the urgency with which it will be dealt. Perception is complicated by issues such as individual tolerance, anxiety and concern about the child himself, fear and anger that the child is behaving in that manner, as well as external pressure from parents, members of the public and, in some situations, the police.

Broadly speaking, behaviour problems will fall into two main categories, those which cause harm to the child, to other children, to adults or to the environment, and those which cause no actual harm. Within each group are behaviours which can be described as additional to the child's learning difficulty and those which are considered so extreme that they must be dealt with.

Aggressive behaviours, such as biting, hitting, scratching or kicking, would come into the first category of being totally unacceptable because of the danger they cause and harm they do. The young person behaves in such a way that an adult or another child is hurt and, in addition, makes people frightened of him. Or the child may cause himself physical injury through hitting or biting himself. Such behaviours will vary in intensity according to the size and strength of the child concerned, but even a small child can hurt if he sinks his teeth into an arm. Dangerous behaviours, such as setting fire to things, extreme bullying, lack of awareness of cause and effect in relation to danger, riding a bike or running straight out into the road for example, will also come into this area.

Behaviours of the second group can be perceived as more acceptable because they do no actual harm to the child, to adults, or to other children, except, of course, to stop the child from learning, for example, rocking, twiddling obsessionally, chewing clothing, swearing and being verbally abusive. Behaviours such as destroying playthings, tearing down displays, upturning toy boxes, taking other people's possessions and non-compliance can be included in this group.

Behaviours of the first broad group are often so physically unpleasant that they are difficult or impossible to live with; those of the second, whilst being socially unacceptable, irritating and unpleasant, can be lived with and are often seen as a natural part of the child; as a result, in some settings, they are often ignored. Harmful behaviours, understandably, tend to cause the most anxiety and more often elicit a crisis-style response from all those concerned.

The above summary illustrates the wide range of behaviour problems displayed by children; it will also have indicated that some behaviours will be easier for the teacher to contemplate than others and that the individual's tolerance levels will be vital in managing the child. In addition, the child's size, strength and age will directly affect the acceptability of the behaviour, as will the setting in which it occurs.

These behaviours will be described in greater detail in the next two sections.

The following views represent two main outline approaches to working with children with behaviour problems and learning difficulties.

View 1

Problem behaviour can been seen as the symptom of an illness or underlying cause from within the child. Attempts are made to 'treat the illness' or remove the cause of the problem and so cure the behaviour problem. It is the child who is seen as the problem and the assumption is that, if the part of the child that is not working properly is dealt with, everything will become straightforward and quickly solved. It is assumed that, by following a course of treatment away from the classroom with an expert, there should be a marked improvement in the child's behaviour, if not a total cure. This view has the following implications for the teacher and for the child:

- First, and most importantly, the problem is seen to come from within the child and is not the teacher's responsibility. Little attention is focused on teacher attitude, expectation, organisation or management skills, or on the factors within the school which can affect learning difficulties and behaviour problems. In this model, the fault is in the child, who is seen to have something wrong with him, rather than in the way he is being taught. This belief leads to the teacher's expectation that someone else must solve the problem and that the child must be removed elsewhere for 'treatment'.
- It reinforces the assumption that the child has an 'illness' which needs to be cured. As the medical and not the teaching profession is responsible for treating illness, there is a risk of returning to the pre-1971 days when children with severe learning difficulties had their learning needs met under the Health Service because they were not considered sufficiently able to benefit from education.
- There is a risk that the teacher may rationalise the problem by having low expectations of the child's behaviour and learning because he has already been labelled as having problems. The process of labelling leads to the problem of the self-fulfilling prophecy: the child will behave inappropriately; the teacher will be looking for problems and is likely to respond negatively to the child; the child will behave badly.
- Traditional teacher training has not prepared teachers for meeting the needs of children with behaviour problems or learning difficulties and, therefore, teachers are more likely to believe that the child's needs cannot and should not be met in the ordinary classroom situation.
- The traditional secrecy and separateness of the treatment process has led to anxiety and concern on the part of teachers that a specialist is needed because of the skills he has to offer.

Consequently, when faced with seemingly intractable problems, the class teacher refers the child for outside help. If that help is forthcoming, it often results in the child's being removed, either temporarily or permanently, from the base class situation. The teacher is then less involved with meeting the child's needs in the classroom setting, the child is isolated from peers and is increasingly seen to be different.

View 2

The second main approach to the management of children with behaviour problems rests on the belief that behaviour is learnt and relates to the context in which the child finds himself. Therefore, any change to the behaviour needs to be in the normal class or home setting. For change to be long lasting and generalised to all settings, all the adults who work with the child need to be involved in the development of more appropriate behaviour. The child's behaviour takes place within a social group of which the adult is a member. It is the interactions between the child, his family, adults and peers that affect his learning and therefore his behaviour rather than something from within himself.

The implications of this view for the child, his peers, and the adults living and working with the child can be summarised as follows:

If behaviour is the result of learning, then appropriate behaviour can be taught in the place of inappropriate behaviour.

The consequences of behaviour will have an important effect on whether the behaviour is repeated and consolidated. People learn generally by repeating behaviour that has had rewarding consequences (going to work in the first week of a job is rewarded by a wage packet and therefore there is a good reason for going in the next week). Children are more likely to work hard if their efforts are valued and if they see some success. A negative response from the adult to a piece of work will reinforce any feeling of inadequacy and perhaps frustration, if the child feels that he has done his best.

The setting in which a behaviour occurs will affect the way in which it is seen and therefore the response it receives. If the child's behaviour is acceptable for the situation in which it occurs, it will be reinforced by a smile, or a 'well done' or some other positive sign that the way he is behaving is appropriate. The child therefore learns not only which behaviours are acceptable but also when and where to display those behaviours. At the same time, inappropriate behaviours may be greeted with an unenthusiastic response, or with punishments or reprisals.

The self-fulfilling prophecy can of course be used positively so that the teacher's expectations of a class or individual child lead to an improvement in general behaviour and achievement. High expectations do not in themselves improve behaviour, but they certainly lead to a positive self-monitoring and evaluation by the teacher and, as importantly by the pupils themselves. High expectations of achievement and behaviour result in an increase in self-esteem, confidence and success.

The adults will be aware that their own behaviour, attitudes and expectations will have an effect on the child and on his behaviour and therefore will be prepared to modify their own approach to help the child. The possibilities of helping and supporting the child are within reach of the teacher or parent, and not just in the hands of an expert.

This model relies on the adults in the child's life being able to share responsibility for helping him, recognising the need for help from others, and learning not only a range of approaches and strategies that work but also having the confidence to try again if the first approach does not work. The view that a shared approach to managing children with behaviour problems is too time-consuming, because it reduces the time and attention given to other children or siblings, is erroneous; children with additional or extreme behaviour problems demand and receive a disproportionate amount of adult or parental attention anyway—that attention might as well be organised to help the child rather than merely to contain him.

KEY POINTS

- The way the behaviour problem is seen will directly affect the urgency with which it is dealt.

- Some behaviour problems are so extreme that they cause physical harm; others can be accepted and tolerated more easily, depending on the age, size and strength of the child and the setting in which the behaviour occurs.

- Tolerance levels, experience and attitude of adults will affect their ability to cope with a child or class or children with behaviour problems.

- It is more useful to the child for adults to accept responsibility for meeting his behavioural and learning needs in the normal classroom or home setting, rather than in isolation from his peers.

- Behaviour is learnt; what a child does can be seen as the result of his interactions with others rather than of inborn characteristics. This applies equally to appropriate and inappropriate behaviour.

7 *Additional behaviour problems*

Any child could be described as having behaviour problems at different times during his education, for example, the child who talks too much in class, the child who kicks a football through a window or the child who is always last in from play. What constitutes an additional behaviour problem? Additional to what? Clearly, additional to the problems that 'normal' children of the same age and ability display. In this context, additional behaviour problems are those behaviours over and above the norm to be expected from children with learning difficulties. For example, a child with severe learning difficulties who has difficulty with continence may be excused for soiling, but would be considered to have an additional behaviour problem if he smeared faeces. A child of the same age in a mainstream school would probably be considered to have a behaviour problem if he were to soil in class.

Behaviour problems seen as additional to the child's learning difficulties are often those which make him stand out from his peers in the first place. They are as likely to be seen in the mainstream classroom as they are in the special school classroom; some of these behaviours will seem far more difficult to cope with in the mainstream classroom because of the number of children and the wide range of ability. Special school teachers have traditionally had to learn to cope with behaviour problems over and above the child's handicap, and are therefore often more confident about managing the child than a mainstream school teacher.

For the sake of clarity the behaviour problems have been grouped; clearly, the groups are not discrete but are intended to show the wide range of difficulties an adult might expect to meet in any class setting. Many problems listed here could be included in different sections according to:

The *duration* of the behaviour
The *frequency* of the behaviour
The *intensity* of the behaviour
The *age, size or strength* of the child
The *setting* in which the behaviour occurs

Additional behaviour problems

a Behaviours which prevent the child from learning in the present setting

Turns round in class
Rocks on chair
Walks round classroom
Ignores instructions

Talks and mutters to self
Pulls faces at others
Asks for constant reassurance
Asks for constant reminders of task
Lifts table with knees
Bangs on table
Interrupts teacher talking
Makes distracting noises out loud
Fidgets with apparatus
Gazes into space
Day dreams
Avoids eye contact
Resists attempting new tasks
Does not have materials needed for class
Does not ask for help
Loses concentration for task in hand
Does not answer questions in a group
Does not listen to reprimands
Does not take criticism
Fails to make friends
Lacks motivation and interest
Refuses to attend school regularly

b Behaviours which are disruptive and therefore unacceptable to others

Enters room noisily
Disrupts start of lesson
Calls out answers
Makes irrelevant comments
Interferes with other people's work
Shouts out to others
Verbally teases and taunts others
Damages other people's property
Steals other children's belongings
Disrupts eating arrangements
Disrupts other children's play or games
Has outbursts of temper

c Behaviours which are anti-social or offensive to others

Swears at adults
Swears at other children

Dribbles continuously
Exposes self to others
Leaves toilet door open when using it
Touches genitals in public
Masturbates in public
Touches other children in a sexual manner
Touches adults in a sexual manner
Spits on furniture or down clothing
Spits at people*
Urinates in inappropriate places *
Soils deliberately *
Smears faeces *
Regurgitates food*

* These behaviours have also been included in the section on behaviours likely to put others at risk because of their potential health risk.

d Behaviours which are likely to place the child at risk either emotionally or physically

Plays truant from school
Absconds from the classroom
Absconds from the playground
Climbs without fear
Does not respond to own name
Refuses to come when called
Mixes with an older peer group
Physically picks on older peers
Indiscriminately talks to strangers
Is over friendly with adults

e Behaviours which are likely to place other children or adults at risk

Mixes with a younger peer group
Instigates misbehaviour in others
Fights with other children
Runs around corridors
Uses equipment in a dangerous manner
Brings dangerous items to school
Bullies other children
Spits at other people *
Soils deliberately *

Smears faeces *
Regurgitates food *
Urinates in inappropriate places *

* see note for section c.

f Behaviours which result in damage to property

Is clumsy with equipment
Damages materials and furniture
Breaks windows
Defaces books, walls and furniture
Chews equipment
Bites equipment
Throws equipment and furniture
Throws food and drink
Leaves taps running

KEY POINTS

- Behaviour problems seen as additional to the child's learning needs can be those which make him stand out from his peers.

- Additional behaviour problems will be found in any setting, main-stream, special class, unit or school, home or in public.

- Additional behaviour problems will be considered more or less extreme according to their duration, intensity and frequency.

- The age, strength and size of the child will affect the seriousness of the problem.

8 Extreme behaviour problems

The most extreme behaviours displayed by a minority of children will rarely be seen by the majority of teachers, but it is important that all people working with children have some idea of the range of difficulties that children face, if only to define clearly the problems as they occur.

There is a close relationship between what are described here as extreme behaviour problems and the additional behaviour problems of the previous section. The division, although somewhat false in terms of category, has been made deliberately to illustrate the two effects: first, the effect the behaviour itself can have on the child's likelihood of being accepted, and, second, the effect that an individual's ability to cope with or tolerate the behaviour will have on the perception of its severity. This is further complicated by the fact that behaviours are seen as more or less extreme according to the setting in which they occur. Many children who display the most extreme behaviours have a whole range of unacceptable behaviours which need somehow to be prioritised in order to be worked with. These complicated groups of behaviours displayed at the same time increase the adult's anxiety and therefore are perceived as extreme.

As with additional problems, the most extreme behaviour problems have been grouped into broad areas; these do, of course, overlap and some children will display problems from each group. Duration, intensity and frequency of the problems will affect the adult's perception of the seriousness of the problem in the same way as with additional problems.

The most extreme behaviour problems that can be identified are those that cause injury to the child or to others.

a Behaviours which may result in the child seriously injuring or mutilating himself

Bangs head with hand
Bangs head on wall
Slaps face with hand
Bites own body, drawing blood
Scratches own body, drawing blood
Picks at existing sores
Rubs skin raw
Pulls hair from head
Pokes eyes with fingers
Pokes eyes with objects
Self induces vomit
Holds breath excessively
Pinches own body, drawing blood
Climbs and jumps from unsafe heights
Rocks against hard surfaces

Note It is difficult to differentiate between behaviours which are self-mutilatory and those behaviours in the next section which are obsessional and stereotypic, but which may result in injury. Often, obsessional behaviours which are extreme lead to physically aggressive outbursts from the child, if an attempt is made to break the obsession. The result of the behaviour can therefore cause additional management problems.

b Behaviours which are obsessional

Rocks body repetitively
Flaps hands
Wrings hands
Flicks fingers
Masturbates continuously
Self induces vomit
Spits and plays with spittle (risk of infection)
Plays with faeces (risk of infection)
Puts hands down throat causing regurgitation (risk of infection)
Runs up and down
Flaps or flicks anything being held
Throws anything put in hand
Cries continuously
Screams continuously
Positions body bizarrely
Sniffs glue/aerosols

c Behaviours that are physically aggressive towards adults or children

Pushes others by surprise
Scratches others, drawing blood
Claws at eyes
Butts with head
Throws objects at people
Bites, drawing blood or causing bruising [high risk of infection, eg. hepatitis B]
Punches others in the face
Punches others on the body
Kicks indiscriminately
Kicks deliberately
Throws furniture
Pulls hair, sharp tugs
Pulls hair, wraps fingers round and will not let go
Uses objects as weapons, eg. scissors
Strangles using clothing
Strangles using hands
Lashes out indiscriminately, using any of the above

Note When a child responds aggressively in desperation, any of the above behaviours may be apparent and it would not necessarily be possible or indeed appropriate to identify individual behaviours except from a safety and preventive point of view. Some children will have learnt to use one or two of the above behaviours in certain settings for a desired result and therefore clear identification would be vital in order to plan a suitable management programme.

Some behaviours on their own are so potentially dangerous that adults need to know if the child is likely to engage in them for their own protection. Generally, adults will know the range of extreme behaviours exhibited by individual children and will have worked out ways at least to contain the child without allowing him to damage anyone else. An understanding of the types of adult- or other-child-initiated behaviour that may trigger dangerous outbursts would be essential.

d Behaviours that demand that the child has constant supervision to ensure safety

Lights fires
Runs into the road
Plays with electricity sockets
Breaks windows, using body
Breaks windows, using a missile
Sleeps irregularly and gets up at night
Wets and soils the bed
Eats anything that can be put in the mouth
Behaves unpredictably and dangerously
Absconds but gets lost
Runs indiscriminately
Hyperventilates

This section could also include any of the above. It may be that the child has no knowledge or understanding of danger, or it could be that he is unable to control himself on some occasions, or that he acts deliberately.

KEY POINTS

- The most extreme behaviour problems are apparent only in a minority of children.
- Often children will display a wide range of problems; the more complicated the range of behaviours displayed, the more extreme the problem will be perceived to be.
- The duration, frequency and intensity of the behaviour(s) will affect the seriousness of the problems.
- The most extreme problems will be those which cause injury to the child, another child or to an adult;

- Children displaying extreme behaviour problems of the type described will require close supervision and constant support.

9 Seeking outside help

Initially, it is important to accept the principle that each teacher should be working as part of a team; it is the responsibility of the Head and senior staff in a school to ensure that reliable support systems are in place. At the same time, class teachers need encouragement to ask for help and support without feeling inadequate and experiencing a sense of failure.

Once such a system is established, the lines of support outside the classroom will become clearer and the question of who to go to for help and when to seek help will be clarified to meet the demands of the individual school or unit.

A school which operates a system of support and monitoring will quickly pick up potential difficulties and make arrangements to manage those problems before crisis point has been reached. Many children have to demonstrate repeatedly that they are having serious problems before anything is done, resulting in feelings of failure and often entrenched negative behaviour patterns. More effective use of early identification skills in relation to potential problems will highlight difficulties at a stage when preventive and ameliorative action can be taken. This applies to the school as well as to the individual class teacher.

There needs to be a whole-school approach to meeting the behavioural as well as the learning needs of the children on roll. Chapter 4 deals with the whole-school approach in detail, but it is necessary here to explore the range of support servics available to the class teacher and to the parents of a child who displays additional or extreme behaviour problems.

Different agencies have different roles and it is necessary to establish links with a range of agencies so that a network of support is available to the school, to the class teacher and to the parents. It is the responsibility of the Head and senior staff to establish those links by encouraging other professionals into the school, by reporting concerns and difficulties clearly and by assessing the needs of pupils, parents and staff in advance whenever possible. This will allow support services to plan their intervention rather than have to respond to crisis. In the same way, the school's development plan should include attention to provision for supporting children with behaviour problems and learning difficulties and incorporate details of the in-service training on offer to staff and parents.

Support services outside the school are never in as good supply as is required. Yet, for the majority of children, including those with behaviour problems, help and support should be available within the school. The support and guidance for the class teacher should be available from some of the following people:

Classroom assistants and welfare attendants
Volunteers
Colleague teachers
Head of department
Members of the senior management team
Deputy head
Head teacher
Educational psychologist
Parents

The school as a whole should be able to look for support and guidance from any of the following services:

Education welfare service
LEA inspectorate/advisorate
Special needs support services
School psychological services
Health services
Social services departments
Community mental handicap team
Probation services
Child guidance

Different geographical areas will have varying suppport services, with some groups taking a special interest in the difficulties of children with behaviour problems. Recent attention by the media has led to increased interest from many professional services in supporting such children in as normal an environment as possible, and considerable work has been done on the more extreme behaviour problems. It could be argued that it is the children with less severe learning difficulties who need additional attention at this time because it is these children who are often seen as trouble-makers, who should know better.

KEY POINTS

- Each school should ensure there is a well structured support system for staff working with children with additional and extreme behaviour problems.

- An appropriate system of support will ensure the early identification of potential problems.

- A whole school approach is vital to supporting children with behaviour problems.

- External support services are available, but should not be expected to 'solve' the problem in isolation from the school.

3
What can be done?

Introduction

The following sections will suggest practical activities and strategies that can be used in a wide range of settings. The broad ability range of the children being considered will mean that some approaches may be more appropriate for some children than for others. It is a deliberate policy to present the strategies and approaches together to reinforce the principle of the continuum of learning difficulties and the complexity of many problems being faced by teachers in mainstream and special classrooms today. Some aspects of each section will be applicable in all school settings and many will relate closely to the home; it will be for the reader to select the principles, approaches and techniques most suitable and useful for their own setting.

Critics of the Elton Report suggested that the Committee could have 'forged more realistic and practical tools for restoring peace and calm to the classroom' (*Education*, March 1989) instead of offering such a wide range of recommendations that affect everybody concerned with schools. The emphasis of this chapter is deliberately practical; aiming to describe many of the tools demanded above, by providing teachers and parents with basic and manageable strategies. The wider implications outlined in the Elton Report will be explored more fully in relation to their practical application in the following chapters.

Part 1

1 Avoiding and preventing problems

It is obviously preferable to avoid problems rather than having to deal with them. Prevention is the best form of intervention with all potential problems. Children with behaviour problems, as we have seen, often behave better with some adults than with others, just as children with learning difficulties may make better progress with some teachers than with others. The way in which the teacher works and behaves with pupils affects the behaviour of the individual child and the class as a whole. Whilst not all problems exhibited by children are the result of teacher or adult behaviour, some problems can be avoided, prevented or minimised if a number of basic rules and approaches are kept in mind.

a Clarify rules and set expectations

It is essential to establish a few basic but important rules for the classroom. Children need and like to know what is expected of them and 'how far they can go', and, of course, as in all aspects of life, rules and their enforcement promote order and predictability. Once the rules are set up, the children will need to be reminded of them, more frequently for very young children, and less frequently as they grow older. The class rules will become part of the overall school rules which will be discussed further in the next chapter.

It is essential for each teacher to make his expectations clear from the outset in order to avoid problems developing through confusion, indecision and insecurity. An expectation of children walking into the classroom quietly and sitting down in their own seat immediately, of moving round the classroom in an orderly fashion and of waiting quietly for instructions and directions, will lead to a calm and positive start to a lesson. Undoubtedly, the more disturbed the children, the more they will need to be reminded of such expectations and the more consistent the adults will need to be in implementing basic expectations. By avoiding problems caused by lack of routine and inconsistent expectation the adult will free time to concentrate on more complex behaviours. The adult will also be far less stressed and therefore be able to respond in a more positive fashion to the efforts made by the children.

Rules for acceptable noise levels will do much to decrease pressure on children and adults alike. Letting children 'call out' in response to questions or to ask for help not only increases the overall noise level in the classroom, but also prevents quieter and less assertive children from attracting the teacher's attention. Many teachers will describe their concern for the child who is quiet and non-demanding in a class where there are children with behaviour problems, usually in terms of that child receiving less teacher time. A general expectation that all children will put their hands up when asking for help, and will wait their turn quietly will lead to a more even distribution of teacher attention.

The way adults use their voices in the classroom will also affect the overall noise level. Adults, who tend to have loud voices anyway, will need to pay close attention to the effect that they have on groups of children. Shouting should generally be avoided as, after a time, the children will no longer listen. The more the adult shouts, the higher the noise level in the room, because the louder the children will have to be in order to hear or to be heard. It is often useful, when observing colleagues, to notice the effects that different uses of the voice have on children. Watch the quiet group of children who are listening to an adult; you will probably note that the adult has something interesting to say and is speaking in a calm and quiet way. The teacher who is demonstrating lack of control will often resort to shouting in an attempt to regain that control. As an occasional strategy it may well work; it certainly will not work as a normal way of communicating with children.

Teachers who work with another adult in the room will need to address the question of what is expected of that adult's behaviour. Many inexperienced teachers in special schools find the task of developing positive working relationships with another adult one of the most stressful aspects of organising the class.

Increasingly, mainstream teachers will meet this problem, as children with special needs are given extra adult support in mainstream classrooms. Often classroom assistants have worked with the children for many years and have seen numerous new teachers through the school. They will have a wealth of experience to offer, but that experience may well intimidate new and inexperienced teachers. This unintentional difficulty needs to be considered when establishing classroom rules and expectations, and will be far easier to deal with if the teacher is clear about his expectations. A clearly defined working relationship will avoid the temptation of children to try to play one adult off against another and will allow consistent management and organisational strategies to be implemented.

The child with additional behaviour problems has often lost a framework of rules and is unsure of what is expected of him. At the same time, he is likely to have met inconsistency from the range of adults in his life and therefore will push the rules to see if it is possible to break them. It is important to re-establish that framework of rules with the children, making clear the reasons for the rules and what will happen if they are broken. There are times when it is necessary to tell children to 'do something, because I say so!' for expediency, but it is much more satisfactory to explain why a rule or decision has been made. Even children with severe learning difficulties can be taught or shown why basic rules have been implemented. Children who deliberately break rules or who are unable to follow rules will need different structures and supports to ensure their safety and the safety of others. Strategies for such children will be described in detail further in this chapter.

With many children it is possible and also desirable to draw up and agree rules together, in order to give them the opportunity to take responsibility for the standards of behaviour in their classroom and school. It is interesting to note how children and adults come up with roughly the same basic rules when given the opportunity to think about what is important to them. Emphasis is usually upon:

Safety of self and others
Respect for and care of others
Looking after own and others' belongings
Trying hard and doing one's best
Doing as one is told

Once the rules have been established, they need to be *displayed* in the classroom for the children to use. It will also be useful for any other adults coming into the room to see the rules that have been agreed. This is particularly true with supply teachers or colleagues taking the class in a temporary capacity and can be a useful device for sharing information with other adults such as classroom assistants and therapists. Attention needs to be paid to the way the rules are displayed, particularly for children with limited reading ability; pictures and diagrams can convey the same information in an interesting and usable form. Competitions amongst the children in the class for the most interesting slogans and posters can help children to feel involved in the task of establishing and agreeing the rules for their class.

b Be prepared

The question of preparation is often discussed in relation to teachers who have difficulty managing children with behaviour problems. Usually it is discussed in terms of lack of preparation and therefore carries an implied criticism of the teacher's lack of commitment or motivation to get things ready for the children. For that reason, there can be a temptation for teachers to avoid examining the effects of good preparation on pupil performance and behaviour. Being prepared to work with and teach children involves thinking ahead and making sure that potential problems are prevented or minimised. It is an area that should be considered by all teachers, because attention to detail and forward thinking can considerably improve the working relationships in the classroom.

Preparation of equipment before the lesson will include checking to see that audio/visual equipment is in working order, testing out practical activities to ensure they work, making sure there are enough pencils to go round and that the pencil sharpener is available in the classroom. All of these may seem obvious, but each could result in a problem if not attended to, particularly if the children involved have short attention spans, are easily distracted or lacking in motivation to work.

The organisation of that equipment is just as important; older children can be given responsibility for looking after their own books, pencils, rubbers, etc, but younger children will need far more supervision. Equipment needs to be stored in an easily accessible place, with contents well marked, and organised so that children can reach without knocking into each other or the furniture. Even very young children and those with limited ability can be taught to put things away in the right place as long as everyone knows where that place is.

Careful attention to lesson plans and making sure all the equipment and apparatus needed for the session is available in the classroom will guard against the teacher having to leave the room in the middle of the lesson to collect something. Often children are sent on errands in the middle of lessons and are in danger of getting into problems whilst out of the room, not least by disturbing another group of children in a different area of the school.

The difficulties faced by supply teachers highlight many of the areas which need to be examined in relation to avoiding problems made worse by lack of attention to preparation. Often supply teachers merely 'cover' a class, unless teaching notes and appropriate equipment and apparatus are obviously available. This lack of continuity undoubtedly leads to increased problems from disturbed children. Supply teachers often have to 'think on their feet' and therefore carry a range of activities that may be appropriate for the age group they are to teach; they need to be flexible and able to assess a situation immediately. Careful preparation of the classroom and appropriate provision of relevant work and activities will ensure the class receives as much continuity as possible in the absence of the regular teacher. Some schools have a system of class files which show the scheme of work being undertaken in each area, by every group or individual child, as appropriate. This relates to the timetable which is displayed on the wall of the classroom. Other schools have individual programmes available in the classroom for each child, stored with a selection of relevant equipment in a tray or drawer. Such a system would be useful for young children or those who have particular learning difficulties. Older, or more able pupils would need to take more responsibility for the retention of their own work, but the preparation and organisation of the work remains the responsibility of the teacher.

Careful attention to preparation will result in a smooth reception of the children into the classroom. Many problems occur at the start of a lesson when the children do not know what is expected of them. It is important to be prepared to start work quickly before losing the attention of the class. Again, simple preparation avoids the development of distraction and disruption. Punctuality on the part of the teacher is a good model for the children; it is as important at the end of a lesson as at the beginning, so that children are not late for the next teacher. By arriving on time and having everything ready to start the lesson, the teacher not only avoids problems from developing but indicates his view of the importance of the work.

Being prepared to be flexible is essential. If a lesson is going really badly, it is more appropriate to stop, regain control and either re-start when the children are attending and behaving appropriately or change to a different activity. It is always useful to have a range of activities prepared for such an eventuality, which can then be presented as a means of diverting further problems. Such activities can be used when there is a crisis in the classroom, especially if the children are used to working independently for periods of time.

Part of the preparation and planning task is to do with content; it is important to make sure that enough materials and work are available for the teacher to fill the whole period of the lesson. Running out of material half way through will lead to the teacher 'bluffing' and the children will know it; behaviour problems are likely to follow. The lesson that aims to get through too much material will cause just as many problems if the children are rushed and do not understand what is expected of them. Children with learning difficulties are likely to become frustrated quickly in either of these situations and will show that frustration by negative and often unacceptable responses.

In addition to appropriate preparation for the whole session, attention needs to be paid to ensuring that there is relevant and interesting work available for the child who finishes the set tasks first. Frustration often results when children finish an activity and become bored because there is nothing else to do. Being told to get your maths book out because you have worked fast may not encourage a child to work quickly next time.

Equally, the child who works slowly or struggles with tasks or activities can be in danger of missing out on the activities that are perceived as more enjoyable. This could act as a deterrent to work rather than encouraging the child to try harder or to persevere. Once activities are planned for these two groups of children, they can be shared with the children so that everyone knows how the session will develop.

Careful preparation and attention to detail in advance will go a long way to preventing class-based problems. It will also demonstrate caring and commitment to the children, by valuing their time and the time spent together.

c Look to yourself

As we have seen in previous chapters, the adult's behaviour will have a direct effect on the behaviour of the children, be that positive or negative. In order to avoid problems developing the teacher will need to think about a wide range of his behaviours that may cause problems.

Class relationships between children and adults are based upon trust, and breaking that trust will lead to resentment from children. It is vital that promises that are made to children are kept. If there is any chance of something not happening, the teacher should not promise, but state the intention and warn of any possible things that may prevent it from happening. Similarly, it is essential that children are not threatened with things that cannot or will not be carried out. The teacher who threatens detention as a punishment if the child does not behave and has no intention of supervising that detention will be storing up problems for himself later. The children need to understand the consequences of their actions and rely upon adults responding in a consistent manner.

Generally speaking, it is wise to avoid threatening children, but if threats are used they must be realistic and capable of being followed through. In addition, the teacher must be prepared to implement the threat if the circumstances demand it. For example, if the teacher threatens a child with telling his parents if the child's unacceptable behaviour continues, he must be prepared to do so. The child is unlikely to take the teacher seriously if he threatens an action and is then seen not to follow it through. The issuing of threats can add to confrontations between adults and children, particularly with children who do not want to lose face in front of their peers. The tough response of 'I don't care' is often uttered by a child who, in fact, does care very much but is unable to accept the threat. Such confrontations and resulting problems can be easily avoided if threatening children is also avoided.

It would be far more appropriate to link consequences with the planning of rules as outlined above. If the children know and understand the consequences of breaking rules, they are more likely to try to avoid getting into problems in the first place. The consequences are then not used as a series of threats but as an agreed and understood response to certain behaviours. The consequences will be presented as a statement of fact, ie, if this happens then that will happen. This is, of course, a strong deterrent if the children are fully involved in the formulation of the rules and contribute to discussions on what should happen if those rules are broken. If the behaviours or infringements of class rules continue, it is appropriate for the teacher to point out who is to blame for the consequences being implemented.

Class peer pressure often comes to bear in this situation, by stopping one member from breaking the rules because all the children know what the consequences will be. It removes the decision from the teacher and rests it clearly on the shoulders of the child who is misbehaving. The other children recognise this fact and respond to the offending member. The teacher has avoided the necessity of having to deal with a potentially difficult problem by forward planning and implementing a class structure which allows the children to take responsibility for their own behaviour.

The question of consistency and fairness is one that needs close attention. Children become confused and anxious when the rules are applied inconsistently from one day to the next, and are angry and confused when a child is seen to get away with behaviours that are seen as unacceptable. This is a particularly difficult problem to deal with in a class of children with varied learning difficulties, particularly when some children have additional behaviour problems. The instinctive response from other children is likely to be, 'If he can do it, so can I.' Sharing the reasons for doing something and discussing outcomes with the children will lead to increased understanding of why it is sometimes necessary to treat people differently. Clearly, it is desirable for the teacher to aim to avoid unexpected changes in the way he behaves towards individuals and classes of children.

It is much easier to be fair, when responding to unacceptable behaviours, if the teacher has seen what is going on. The teacher can increase awareness of who caused problems and what actually occurred by moving round the classroom frequently, by seeing situations from different viewpoints and by listening to children instead of making snap judgements. Developing such strategies will guard against the other children behaving inappropriately because they may have been blamed for something they did not do.

Linked to the subject of fairness are the different ways in which teachers react to situations. Over and under-reaction can both lead to increased problems from children with additional behaviour difficulties. A confident and calm manner and a consistent response to problem behaviours will lead to a sense of security in children and reinforce the knowledge that the teacher is in charge and capable of maintaining control. Angry over-reaction to what might be seen as a petty incident can easily increase its importance in the children's eyes. Children respond quickly and negatively to teachers who over-react, and are likely to repeat the behaviours in order to have an opportunity to watch the teacher lose his composure. Added to that, the effect of over-reacting is likely to be an increase in stress and tension for the teacher and little positive effect on the behaviour of the children.

Under-reaction on the part of the teacher can be as likely to lead to an increase in problems of unacceptable behaviour. Quite simply, the children have not been checked. They have not received a response which illustrates whether the behaviour is acceptable or not. (There is, of course, a case for ignoring unacceptable behaviours in some situations, which will be discussed in greater detail later in this chapter.) Problems can often be avoided or minimised if they are 'nipped in the bud'; if the teacher sees a problem developing and diverts the children's attention, the problem may well be avoided. For example, drawing attention to a problem such as a gradual increase in noise level and encouraging children to work more quietly will avoid the need for the teacher to raise his voice to be heard above a riot.

Often problems can be avoided if the style of language used by the adult is changed. For example, children, just like adults, respond badly to being 'bossed about'; they appreciate being asked rather than told and like to have warning of a change of activity. They resist being ordered to do things without a reason and will often refuse, which leads to confrontation. Constant attention to what they are doing wrong serves to reinforce failure and inadequacy rather than to build up desirable behaviours and skills.

The style of language adopted by the teacher will affect the responses from the child. Observations on the use of language by teachers highlight phrases that will be more likely to elicit the desired response from children and avoid and prevent problems from occurring, e.g.

Please will you put your books away.
That's a much better piece of work.
It would help Susan if . . .
Thank you for working so quietly.
Let me show you an easier way to do . . .
In five minutes we will . . .
Would you like some help?
When you have finished . . .
Let's see who is sitting up straight.

Negative, dictatorial or sarcastic use of language will lead to children feeling humiliated, criticised or inadequate. When such phrases are written down, it seems obvious that they may well cause offence or lead to an increase in negative responses from children, eg

I've had enough of you, class 6.
Don't keep playing with your books.
Will you be quiet/shut up/stop shouting.
Right, put everything away and line up.
Well, that looks a mess. Couldn't you do any better?
Put that scrappy bit of work in the bin.
Do you call that creative writing?
You really are stupid, Steven.
Don't bother to come tomorrow if you can't behave.

It is not only the content of adult language that can be modified in order to avoid problems with children but also the intonations and the way things are said. As has already been mentioned, shouting continuously is likely to raise the noise level but, more importantly, will result in children not listening. In an emergency situation it may be necessary to shout as a sharp way of getting children to attend; it will not work if the children are used to shouting. Equally, being rude or sarcastic to children will not give an appropriate model of language for children to copy. Indeed, in the long term it will cause more problems as children respond in a rude and insolent manner with other adults.

Questions to ask

Are my requests reasonable?
Does the child understand what I am asking him to do?
Is he capable of doing what I am asking him to do?
Are my instructions clear?
Do I listen to the children?
Do I ever humiliate the children?
Do I ever interrupt children when they are speaking to me?
Do I explain what we are going to do?
Do I shout too much?
Do I say 'please' and 'thank you' to the children?

Development in skills of self-appraisal will help the teacher to identify the effects that his behaviour will have on the children and will in turn help him to isolate the ones which lead to an increase in negative or unacceptable responses from children. Avoiding and preventing problems by always making a positive effort to demonstrate appropriate styles of behaviour to children is a powerful and often undervalued management strategy.

d Supervise closely

Close supervision from adults does much to minimise and avoid problem behaviour. The physical presence of teachers at unstructured times such as lunch break will in itself lead to a decrease in behaviour problems. If all adults take responsibility for ensuring that the general standards of behaviour are upheld at those times some problems will be avoided.

Individual children will need more or less supervision according to their level of dependence and the severity of their behaviour problems. Children who are self-abusive or aggressive will need close supervision at all times to prevent them from hurting themselves or others. Problems of this nature will be minimised by close supervision because the adult will be able to intervene to prevent the behaviour from occurring. It is easy to see in such an extreme example why supervision is so important.

Children who have a limited sense of danger will require close supervision in certain settings, most obviously, when out in the community near to traffic. By holding the child's hand serious danger in terms of the child running under a car is avoided. Generally, adults are aware of the need for close supervision in such extreme situations because the results of lack of supervision are only too obvious. This becomes less so as children grow older or show that they are more able to look after their own safety.

It is clear, however, that behaviour problems are far more likely to occur when groups of children are together in an unsupervised situation. Avoidance and prevention of problems can only occur if an adult is on hand, ready to step in if a problem looks likely. Leaving a class of children with behaviour problems, even for a short time, is asking for difficulties. The problems outlined in the previous chapter are managed better when the adults concerned work in a structured and supportive manner, in close contact with the children. Knowledge of exactly what is happening in the room at all times will allow early identification of potential problems and give the teacher time to do something to avoid them. The teacher will immediately be able to see those children who are struggling with their work and those who are beginning to be disruptive or non-compliant.

Constant movement around the room lets the children know that the teacher is always aware of what they are doing. They are therefore less likely to start behaving in unacceptable ways. Similarly, close supervision when children are moving from one lesson to another, coupled with a clear expectation of how they will move through the school, will minimise behaviour problems.

Children can also be supervised from a distance with structures being imposed as part of the monitoring of their behaviour. For example, parents cannot be expected to supervise their children at all times, particularly when the children go out independently; they can, however, lay down expectations on how they should behave when they are out and when they should return. This monitoring shows that the parents care about what the child does and that they expect them to behave in an appropriate manner.

The Elton Committee recognised the serious problems faced by many schools during the midday break, when children are largely supervised by untrained dinner supervisors. The Report recommended that teachers be encouraged to take on a supervisory role at midday because of their experience in the management of behaviour problems. The Committee also recognised the dilemma faced by teachers who do not contractually have to supervise children at midday breaks. Many schools have been so concerned about the seriousness of behaviour problems during the poorly supervised break period that teachers have decided to return to a rota of dinner-time supervision. This has been true particularly of teachers working with children who have learning difficulties and additional behaviour problems, because it has been felt that much valuable work is undone during unstructured times. By increasing structured supervision at lunch-time many problems are being avoided.

e Maximum use of resources

The word 'resources' in this context applies to time, personnel, furniture and fittings as well as equipment and apparatus. Careful attention to the use of resources at the teacher's disposal will point to ways of preventing and avoiding behaviour problems.

The organisation of time through the class timetable should take into account not only the balance and breadth of curriculum areas to be covered, but also the proximity of subjects. For example, a day made up of largely sedentary, academic subjects will put children under more pressure than a day that is balanced between practical and active learning opportunities. It is important that the curriculum for children with learning difficulties should be as practical as possible; many may argue that the curriculum for all children should be as practical as possible. The balance of time spent in each subject area and the organisation of sequence of subjects will depend upon the age and abilities of the children concerned, but should always be considered when looking to avoid behaviour problems.

Turning to the question of personnel, we have seen some of the potential difficulties, particularly for inexperienced teachers, when working with other adults in the classroom; the advantages of having support and developing a team approach to working with the children should outweigh the difficulties. Increasingly, parents are being encouraged to work alongside teachers in classrooms, giving additional help and support to children. Parents and other members of the community can be included in the class team and can make a positive contribution to the work going on in the classroom. Difficulties arise when the class rules are not made explicit and parents do not share the same goals and expectations as teachers. The vital thing here is to ensure good communication between teachers and parents through making regular opportunities for discussion. Information available in the classroom on the work that individuals and groups are undertaking, clear and well presented timetables and, if appropriate, behaviour management strategies and programmes will all serve to inform parents and other adults of the expectations on the class.

Should problems arise with a particular child, the availability of other adults will enable the teacher to organise activities that can be continued whilst he manages the difficulty. With training or guidance, the other adult can be asked to take the individual child into another area of the classroom, or even to another area of the school to help the child sort out his problems. This will prevent the child's behaviour having a negative effect on the other children and will allow them to get on with their work in a settled and positive way. Often the focus of individual attention on the child who is displaying the behaviour problem will lead to a decrease in the problem; it will almost certainly avoid other children joining in.

Sharing information and discussing difficulties with both senior and junior colleagues will often show ways of working that will avoid problems, or at least throw a new light on the difficulties being experienced. Using the skills and knowledge of parents will often highlight potential problems and give ideas on how to avoid problems with their children. Adults in this context are a resource to 'use' and to learn from; it is true that a new person coming into a situation will often see a way to avoid a problem the next time. It is sometimes difficult for the teacher to ask for or accept such observations in a positive manner. It is, however, essential for the teacher of children with additional behaviour problems to learn to ask for help, in the confidence that he is not alone in the struggle to manage the complex needs of his pupils.

Furniture can be used to minimise and avoid problems with a group of children. Decisions on seating can be important in avoiding or minimising problems. First, attention needs to be given to group dynamics and the opportunity children have for irritating, teasing or hurting each other. The way the chairs are set out can cause or minimise problems of this nature. It doesn't take much time to work out the children in a class who do not leave each other alone or who cause problems because they are together. Careful use of positioning can avoid unnecessary disruption. In some situations it is necessary to keep the most unsettled child next to the teacher, either to help him stay on task or to stop him from wandering. The expectation would be that, in time, he would be able to work appropriately with less supervision or support.

Tables, chairs and desks need to be positioned in such a way that all the children can see the teacher or the main focus of attention, such as a display board. If children cannot see what is going on or cannot hear, they are likely to become distracted and problems will occur. Particular care needs to be taken with seating children who are partially sighted or partially hearing, and maximum use should be made of available audio/visual aids.

Children who are easily distracted need to work in a stimulus-free area. Furniture can be used to block off an area in the classroom so that a child or small group of children can work away from the main class. It is also useful when teaching a child who disrupts others by obsessional movements or constantly standing up. The furniture becomes a secure area where the child can work calmly without being reinforced in inappropriate behaviour by the other children.

The planned use of space is as important when aiming to avoid or minimise behaviour problems as the use of furniture within the classroom. Attention needs to be paid to the paths available for children to move from their seat to, for example, the teacher or to the book corner.

Potential problems can be avoided by decreasing the obstacles in the path of children. If different children have different paths to follow congestion will be avoided on 'busy' routes. The same attention will need to be paid to routes from one room to another, as the movement of children around the classroom or the school is likely to lead to problems if there is little organisation or structure.

In the most extreme situation, furniture can be used as a barrier between a child displaying physically aggressive behaviour and the focus of that aggression, whether child or adult. This would only be an immediate response to a potentially dangerous situation and, if it looked as though the child was determined to be violent towards another person, other strategies would need to be used to ensure safety. Physical restraint and alternative tactics to avoid violent situations will be explored in more detail below. Often, the use of a cupboard or table to separate the child from the teacher for a few moments will allow enough time for the adult to calm the situation.

In less serious situations, furniture can be used to slow a child down; it is often suggested by teachers that small classrooms lead to an increase in hyperactive behaviour in some children. In my experience, the opposite is true. A large area does not give a child who is constantly moving any physical framework in which to control his behaviour. On the contrary, if he has too much space he is likely to find difficulty in settling to an activity. By using furniture to divide the classroom into areas for different activities, or for different groups of children, it is possible to build in barriers and physical boundaries for hyperactive children, so that the build-up of regular or obsessional running and moving around the classroom can be checked at the stage when the child cannot control himself.

If a child climbs obsessionally, the choice and use of furniture will be crucial to avoid accidents and danger. The positioning of furniture in this situation will also be important. For example, putting cupboards in front of windows might provide the ideal stepping-stone for a child who is intent on climbing out. By placing furniture in different positions in the classroom this problem may be avoided or at least contained until an adult can reach the child and prevent the problem occurring. Putting a table or cupboard in front of the direct line to the door could deter a child from absconding or give the adult time to intercept. Furniture used in this way is perceived by the child as a barrier and not as a challenge; the need for confrontation is therefore avoided.

The teacher can store and organise classroom equipment and apparatus in ways designed to avoid problems, making sure that everything has a place and teaching the children to put everything in its place; implicit in this arrangement is a high level of order and tidiness. Clear marking of drawers, cupboards and trays will enable other adults to find things and put them away properly. Adding pictures and simple diagrams to the words can help children to recognise the content of cupboards if they are unable to read or are having difficulty with reading. Problems are avoided in terms of wasting time looking for things, frustration when everything falls out of an untidy or cluttered cupboard, and constant demands for equipment that is not readily available.

The availability of equipment will depend on the particular needs and problems of the children in the class. For example, in a class where children throw things or upturn boxes and trays, it is asking for problems to leave tiny pieces of equipment around, such as beads, lego and counters. Children who use objects as missiles or weapons should not have easy access to scissors and other potentially dangerous items. Staplers, scissors and craft knives should not in any circumstances be left around in any class situation; obviously, as children grow older they need increased access to equipment which could be potentially dangerous if misused but their introduction to such equipment must be in line with their proven ability to respond appropriately to safety rules. This ability does not necessarily keep pace with chronological age.

f Evaluate

Evaluation involves identifying positive strategies and building upon them and minimising areas of difficulty by identifying what went wrong and planning alternative actions for the next occasion. By looking critically at classroom relationships, organisation, presentation and content of the lesson it becomes possible for the teacher to identify the successful and not so successful aspects and therefore avoid problems and difficulties for the future. A written report of a lesson or incident allows the evaluation process to begin. It is useful for the teacher to evaluate his own lessons, expectations and relationships, but opportunities for involving colleagues should be encouraged, as different views can be valuable.

Evaluating successful practice and recording the positive aspects of lessons can help to avoid problems in the future, and can give the teacher positive feedback and encouragement to keep trying. An emphasis on the positive will also help the adult to concentrate on the 'good' things that the children do rather than always look for the problems and difficulties. When it comes to planning an individual programme for a child with behaviour problems it is necessary and advisable to isolate strengths and interests as a starting point; the same applies to planning and implementing a whole-class policy – identify the strengths and use them as the foundation to build upon.

When problems have occurred in a lesson, the ability to evaluate in an objective way, what went wrong can pinpoint avoidance tactics in the future. Often the initial reactions of the teacher after a really traumatic lesson will involve feelings of frustration, anger at himself and/or the children and, undoubtedly, an increase in tension. It is crucial to accept that there will be problems from time to time for all teachers and that skills in self-appraisal and evaluation will help to decrease the pressures by keeping things in perspective. By developing an evaluation system that examines success as well as perceived weakness and failure, the teacher will be able to look objectively rather than emotionally at what has occurred.

Problems will be minimised and avoided in the classroom if teachers manage to pitch work at an appropriate level for the children in the class. An evaluation of the progress made by children will show whether work is too demanding and therefore resulting in frustration and probable failure, or not demanding enough, in which case the children do not experience success and the intrinsic pleasure of achievement. By evaluating work undertaken and responding to the information made available, the teacher will be able to modify his expectations and so minimise unnecessary problems.

Some questions to ask yourself

How do I expect this child to behave?
Does the child behave as I expect?
If not, what have I tried to do to help the child behave as I expect?
Has there been a change in the child's behaviour because of my intervention?
How big a change has occurred?
What form has the change taken?
Is the change a positive one?
If not, what other strategies can I try?
If the child is making progress, is the rate of progress sufficient?
What have I done to help the child make such progress?
Has my expectation been met?

Ongoing evaluation is a formative process leading to an overview of what is happening in the classroom and allowing appropriate modifications of practice to take place. The early identification of problems or potential problems through evaluation and self-evaluation will enable the teacher to change what is happening and thereby avoid or minimise problems.

Where staff are uncertain of their ability to identify particular problem areas, use can be made of a behavioural checklist. Many checklists are produced commercially and caution must be urged in using them, for two reasons. First, there is a temptation to evaluate the behaviour that is listed on the particular programme rather than that which is occurring. Second, there can be massive waste of time in filling in detailed profile sheets in a range of areas where there may be no significant problem.

Such checksheets can, however, provide some support for teachers in the early stages of programme development, and can assist them while they build up their own skills in the area. If such checklists are used there are some key areas which will prove more useful than others.

Behaviour area	Indications of key activities
Relationship with peers	Physical and verbal abuse Provocation Conflict Rejection Play co-operation Ability to give/accept help Lying
Classroom behaviour	In-seat behaviour In-class behaviour In-school behaviour Attendance Punctuality Handling furniture and equipment Level of supervision required Talking/interruption Disruption Attention-seeking
Self perception	Level of self-confidence Awareness of strengths Ability to accept criticism Ability to accept praise Pride in achievement
Relationship with authority	Physical or verbal abuse of adults Lying Provocation in formal and informal school settings Acceptance of school rules Acceptance of punishment

g Prevent escalation

It is essential for the class teacher to avoid and prevent problems from escalating into serious situations. First of all, the teacher needs to recognise that there is a problem, or a potential problem. Many behaviour problems can be dealt with calmly and firmly in the classroom by the teacher responding immediately and fairly to the child or children involved. Being aware of what is going on at all times and avoiding difficulties developing by speedy action will produce a more positive working environment.

The teacher needs to get to know the children so that he is able to recognise potentially difficult conflicts and therefore be ready to deal with them should they occur. It is sometimes necessary to make allowances for children, but the teacher must always make sure that they know where the line is drawn. Children, like adults, have to respond to different expectations and situations all the time, and are often surprisingly able to change their behaviour to suit the setting. It is important for the teacher to be consistent in class to prevent an escalation in, for instance, swearing behaviour.

One of the most commonly used ways of preventing problems from escalating is by stopping the activity and calling for everyone's attention. This is usually used when there is too much noise in the classroom or when some children are causing a minor disturbance. The technique of waiting until everyone is quiet and attending before going on with the lesson will work only if it is used early enough; it will achieve the result of calming the children and allowing the teacher to regain control. An equally useful technique which can be used successfully with younger children is to divert the child's attention from the problem behaviour into a more acceptable activity. For example, the child who is about to throw a bucketful of bricks can be praised for picking it up and being about to put it away, although the adult may need to help the child to put the bucket in the right place, thus stopping him from throwing it.

Problems can escalate when adults argue with children. When the adult behaves in a calm and controlled manner he is able to listen to the problems, make the necessary decisions on how to deal with them and respond appropriately. If, on the other hand, he over-reacts and loses his temper, he may well cause the problem to escalate. Aggression readily leads to further aggression, and an adult who responds to a child in the way that the child is behaving will cause more problems than he avoids. From time to time it may be necessary to ask another adult to take over while the teacher regains control of himself. This is better, for the teacher and the child, than the teacher losing his temper and behaving in an emotional and uncontrolled way. The school must see that the support structures are in place to help teachers if they are coping with children who constantly behave in an aggressive or demanding manner.

It may be necessary to separate children who are arguing, to prevent them from fighting. It will almost certainly be necessary to separate children who are fighting, and sometimes to isolate one child from the other in order to minimise the effect of reinforcement from other children. Such action will allow the children concerned to 'cool off' without being seen to lose face in front of the others. Anyone who has taken playground duty will know how important it is to separate and isolate some children in order to sort out conflicts and problems. It is always easier to defuse problems when talking to one child, or a small group, than when trying to calm a large group of children down.

It is important for adults to recognise the time to ask for help. Help and support should be available from colleagues in potentially serious situations, not just to remove the child who is posing the most problems, but possibly to take the class whilst the teacher manages the problem. In this situation, the adult is seen by the child and by the other children to follow through with the problem and not merely pass it on to someone else. There will be occasions when it is necessary to send or take a child to a senior member of staff, but it is better from the point of view of avoiding problems in the future for the class teacher to deal with the difficulties himself. Such an approach relies on a support structure in the school which incorporates other teachers, both senior and junior, who are able and willing to take over in the classroom.

Clearly, the teacher must respond immediately in a dangerous or potentially dangerous situation. On some occasions it will be necessary to remove the rest of the children from the room. If, for example, the child is too big or acting in a physically violent manner, the teacher will need to make a judgement about the potential risk to the other children. Sometimes the object of the child's violent attention is another child. By removing that child, the teacher will prevent the first child's aggression from escalating and at the same time ensure the safety of all concerned. On rare occasions, the adult may have to deal with a child threatening to attack someone with a dangerous object. The first priority must be the safety of the rest of the children and other adults in the vicinity. After that, the teacher will need to send for help from a senior colleague, staying out of reach of the child. Should the child be throwing furniture or equipment, it may be necessary for the teacher to leave the room, although he should try to talk the child down from outside the door. If the child is not able to calm himself down, he may need to be physically restrained when help arrives. As a general rule, physical force should not be used unless it is absolutely necessary (see *Physical restraint, uses and abuses* below). It is essential in such situations to ensure the safety of all concerned.

h Avoid unnecessary confrontations

One definition of confrontation is deliberately to meet someone face to face in hostility or defiance. It is always used to describe an act of opposition and, in the case of an adult responding to a child, it will inevitably involve the adult's imposing his will over the child in some way or another and is likely to result in the child's resisting. This resistance will be either verbal or physical, for example, walking out, hitting out or throwing something. Everyone will have experienced the situation where the adult tells the child to do something, the child refuses, the adult insists, the child responds with a 'Why should I?' and the adult says 'Because I say so!' and an argument ensues. Such confrontations occur frequently and can result in more or less of a management problem, depending on the ability of the adult to avoid the situation getting out of hand.

The key to this section is to determine when it is necessary to confront a child who is displaying an additional behaviour problem and when it is unnecessary or likely to exacerbate the situation. The teacher needs to recognise those problems which must be dealt with immediately, those which can be played down and those which either can be ignored or dealt with in passing. As usual, factors such as the ability of the child, the age and size of the child and the setting in which the problem behaviour is occurring will inevitably influence the decision. Some general considerations will nevertheless apply.

1 Arguing with children rarely does anything other than make problems worse.
2 Avoid jumping to conclusions – if there is time, listen to what the child has to say and then respond.
3 Take care over phrasing requests – asking a child rather than telling him to do something is more likely to avoid the need to insist.
4 Be prepared to apologise if you have made a mistake. It is as important for the adult to back down when he is wrong as it is for the child.
5 Provide opportunities for the child to repair the problem rather than deal with it head on. For example, help the child to pick up all the beads that have been thrown rather than telling him off and insisting he does it on his own.
6 Stay one step ahead. Avoiding or preventing a child from behaving inappropriately will also avoid the need to confront him for his behaviour.
7 If possible, give the child time to calm down. Often the problem is not as serious as it first seems, and a precipitate response may well make it worse.
8 Give the child space. By removing the attention of adults and children a confrontation can often be avoided.
9 Be confident that you can deal with the problem before confronting the child. Difficulties are likely to escalate if the child knows that you cannot cope. Children need the security of knowing that their behaviour can be managed.

There will be some situations where a confrontation is necessary, but the above points should be borne in mind, to avoid situations getting out of control.

KEY POINTS

- Prevention is the best form of intervention.

- Clear rules and expectations need to be agreed and implemented.

- Careful preparation of lessons, equipment, apparatus and resources will enable teachers to minimise and avoid many behaviour problems.

- Adults need to be aware of the effect of their own behaviour on the behaviour of child.

- The style of language and intonation used will affect the child's response.

- Behaviour problems are far more likely to occur when children are unsupervised; close supervision avoids problems from arising.

- Many problems can be avoided or minimised if attention is paid to choice, organisation and presentation of resources.

- Skills in evaluation and self-appraisal are essential in identifying positive strategies and isolating areas of difficulty.

- Structured evaluation enables the teacher to modify his behaviour and the setting to avoid or minimise problems in the future.

- Many problems can be 'nipped in the bud' before they become serious.

- Confrontations are not always necessary.

2 *The 'ORA' procedure*

The next stage of answering the question 'What can be done?' in relation to working positively and successfully with children who have additional and extreme behaviour problems is to examine the ORA procedure.

The ORA procedure contains three elements:

OBSERVING
RECORDING
ANALYSING

That is, the observation of what is going on with the child, the recording of his behaviour or behaviours, and the analysis of that behaviour or behaviours. The ORA procedure needs to be described before looking at the range of management strategies available, and will need to be incorporated into any successful approach to managing children with behaviour problems.

Accurate and systematic recording is essential in the process of observing and analysing behaviour. Record-keeping systems allow the adult to:

1 Gather information upon which decisions can be made. This information becomes the starting point or 'base-line'.
2 Isolate the desired outcomes for the child.
3 Report accurately to interested people.
4 Work within a pre-planned framework, that is, clarify exactly what is to be recorded before embarking on observation and analysis.
5 Evaluate the effectiveness of management strategies.

Written record-keeping systems can take a number of different forms, but must basically be quick and easy to use, be clear in layout and have sufficient space to include all the essential details. Information can be recorded on audio and video tape in the first instance, and later transferred to the written form. Information on records needs to be clear, precise and easy to read, particularly if it is to be useful to other people. Writing reams of notes may be of use to you if you have time to read them, but they are unlikely to be as valuable to someone else as a summary chart containing the same information. For example, a record of a child's toileting behaviour could be presented as shown on the page opposite.

This form of record-keeping is designed to be completed quickly, with the information to be included clearly stated. It could be adapted according to the information to be collected. It could include an area for comments and might incorporate space for the previous week's record, or for totals. The important aspect of this type of recording is that the chart is designed to focus the attention of the adult completing it on certain pre-decided pieces of information. It is carefully structured to record only specific pieces of behaviour, which can later be analysed to form the base-line of the child's toileting behaviour.

All teachers use a wide range of record-keeping techniques as part of their daily work. They keep records of:

Individual programmes being followed, with space to record progress made and future targets or goals.
Results of tests and assessments, both standardised and not.
A cumulative profile of each child's achievements.
Areas of concern about children's progress and behaviour.

TOILETING RECORD

Name *Sally*   Date record started *12th June*

Key   UT   – Used Toilet
      DRY – Dry when taken [to be taken every hour]
      WET – Wet pants
      S   – Soiled pants

TIME	MON	TUES	WED	THURS	FRI	SAT	SUN
7–8	DRY	S	WET				
8–9	WET	WET	WET				
9–10	WET	DRY	WET				
10–11	UT	DRY	UT				
11–12	DRY	UT	UT				
12–1	S	S	DRY				
1–2	DRY	DRY	S				
2–3	WET	DRY	WET				
3–4	DRY	UT					
4–5	UT	WET					
5–6	DRY	WET					
6–7	DRY	WET					
7–8	UT	DRY					

This chart shows the following information: the times the child used the toilet, the number of times the child had wet or soiled and the most usual times for him to use the toilet.

The planning and evaluation of lessons.
How often things occur, for example the frequency of listening to a child read.
What subjects and areas have been covered, such as topics.
Attendance.

These records may be presented in a chart format such as:

Names	4.4	5.4	6.4	7.4	8.4	11.4	12.4	13.4	14.4	15.4	18.4	19.4
John S	√	√	√	√			√					
Peter	√		√	√	√	√	√					
Sue	√	√	√	√	√		√					
Mark	√	√	√	√	√	√	√					
Anne	√	√	√			√	√					

Other records will be written descriptions of what has been going on:

> ## Monday 12th June:
>
> Class 4 were very unruly today. They came into the room in a very noisy way and then took at least half of the lesson to calm down to work. Next week, I shall make sure that I meet them at the door and quieten them down *before* they come into the classroom.

Pre-planned lists of teaching outcomes can also form the basis of a recording system that is cumulative,

Money	L.S.	R.H.	D.S.	D.W.	V.W.						
1 Matches coins	√2.6		√4.4	/2.2	/						
2 Sorts coins	√3.7	√5.4									
3 Names coins											
4 Selects coins up to 50p											
5 Reads prices											
/ = working on √ = achieved (add date)											

There are numerous other styles and examples of recording, some of which will be introduced in the next few sections, in order to illustrate ways of gathering information about children's behaviour. Many of these may be familiar to the reader, but can be adapted to the individual setting in which the teacher finds himself. The important thing to remember is that structured and accurate recording systems are an essential part of observing and analysing behaviour.

Key points to record-keeping:
The record is the basis for evaluation.
It should be useful to the teacher.
It should be useful to others.
It should be well organised and well presented.
It should show desired/expected outcomes.
It should show progression.
It should always be dated.
Symbols and abbreviations should be explained.
It should be completed accurately and clearly.

Observing and recording behaviour

The first stage of the ORA procedure is to observe what is going on in the classroom or with a particular child. Information needs to be gathered on:

what the child is doing,
who he is doing it with,
when he is doing it,
where he is doing it,
how long he is doing it,
how serious the behaviour is to the child and to others.

When a teacher has particular problems with an individual child, he needs to focus his attention on the range of problems the child is exhibiting and on the positive aspects of the child's behaviour. One way of starting this process is to write a description or 'pen picture' of the child and the range of things he does. The pen picture should answer the following questions:

What sort of behaviours does the child display?
What does he do when he is behaving appropriately?
Does his behaviour affect others or just himself?

Is his behaviour similar to the behaviour displayed by the other children in his class?

The following example of a pen picture was the initial description of a child made by a teacher in a mainstream school:

Christopher

Christopher is twelve years old, big for his age and always seems to be in trouble in school. He is often rude to teachers and is usually late to lessons, walking in noisily and disturbing everyone else. Nobody can do anything with him because he just does not want to learn. His reading is poor and he doesn't seem able to concentrate for very long.

Christopher likes doing art and craft work and will work quietly in cookery, although he is usually late to both lessons as well. He seems to be less ill-mannered when there is a class discussion and usually makes a good contribution. He has lots of good ideas when he is encouraged to talk about them. Christopher disrupts the other children with his messing about. His behaviour also stops him from learning. The other children think he is a bully and don't like him very much – he spends break times with boys in the fifth year.

Such a description will outline a range of starting points. The process of describing the child will be the first step in the teacher's task of observing what is going on in the class. The points that he has noted down will need to be looked at in more detail in order to gather more useful information. For example, the phrase 'always seems to be in trouble at school' is a general impression, which may or may not prove useful when looking at what the child is doing. It may say far more about the adults' behaviour than about the child's.

'He is often rude to teachers' gives little real indication of the sort of behaviour that is causing the problem.

What does he do that is seen as being rude?
How often does he do it?
How many teachers is he rude to?

Questions such as these begin to form when the teacher reads the pen picture. They form even more easily when another adult reads the description and begins to ask, 'What do you mean by . . .?'

The next step is to decide how best to measure the behaviour. If he is 'usually late to lessons', does that mean three out of every ten lessons or nine out of every ten? That is, how serious is the problem and how can the teacher find out the frequency of Christopher's lateness? It is necessary to decide how important the problem is in order to prioritise the behaviour problems for the purposes of implementing management strategies. There are two pieces of information to concentrate on here: first, the frequency of his lateness, and, second, the duration of his lateness – that is, how long after the beginning of the lesson does Christopher arrive?

Observing and recording frequency of behaviour can be a simple process as long as the behaviour to be observed is short-lived and occurs only from time to time. The teacher merely notes down every time the behaviour occurs and ends up with a total. This total will be of use only if there is other information to go with it, for example, in the case of the number of times that Christopher is late for his lessons, the number 23 would be of little use. If the teacher observed and recorded that Christopher was late 23 times out of a possible 30 in one week it would be clear that there was a real problem. In addition to the number of times that Christopher was late, it may be useful to look at the lessons that he arrived early or on time for, as well as to examine those lessons that he was late for. This may raise the question: why is he always late for English and Geography, but on time to Maths? The process of observing and recording frequency of behaviours can therefore give the opportunity to gather information on other areas. The key is to design a chart to be used to record such observations as fully, yet as simply, as possible.

The two charts that follow are examples of the points made. In order to complete the recording process accurately and quickly, the teacher needs to be able to see clearly what must be recorded and where it must fit on the chart (diagram 1). If additional information is required, it is helpful if that is also included (diagram 2).

The totals have been included to show how many asterisks (*) and ticks (√) the child has received on a given day, and at a given time. For example, is Christopher more often late into class after dinner break than first thing in the morning? Is he late more often on some days than on others? How often is he late to dinner? This chart will clearly show how often Christopher has been late to lessons over a period of three weeks. The base-line frequency of his lateness has therefore been established. The gathering of information points the way to what else is needed. For example, are there some lessons that Christopher is always late to and, if so, what are they?

The teacher can complete the timetable and then add the asterisks (*) and ticks (√) as appropriate. In this instance, the totals are less important because the teacher is collecting information about the frequency of lateness relating to individual lessons.

Diagram 1

Name														Date	

* every time the child is late
∨ every time the child is on time

	M	T	W	Th	F	M	T	W	Th	F	M	T	W	Th	F	TOTALS
9.45																
10.30																
11.15																
Dinner Break																
1.00																
1.45																
2.30																
Total																

Diagram 2

Name				Date	

* every time the child is late
∨ every time the child is on time

	MONDAY	TUESDAY	WEDNESDAY	THURSDAY	FRIDAY
Lesson 1					
Lesson 2					
Lesson 3					
BREAK					
Lesson 4					
Lesson 5					
Lesson 6					

This sort of recording is relatively easy to do and often highlights patterns of behaviour exhibited by the child that gives direct pointers to the triggers of the problem. Recording duration of behaviour problems can be more difficult or, by its very nature, more time-consuming.

Duration-recording concentrates on the observed amount of time that the child continues a behaviour. In the example above, it would be necessary to record how many minutes late Christopher is for each lesson. If Christopher is two minutes late for every lesson there is a less serious problem than if he is ten minutes late. Duration-recording will give the necessary information.

Observing and recording of this type can be time-consuming for the teacher because he literally has to time the behaviour. He may spend far more time observing one child than working with the class as a whole. Many teachers find it difficult to observe and time one set of behaviours when they are responsible for a class and, because of the demands of other children, often forget to note down the behaviour being observed. This is where another adult can help. If the teacher sets the observation up and clearly describes the behaviour being timed, the other adult can do the job, leaving the teacher free to continue working with the rest of the children. It need not necessarily be another teacher; parents, classroom assistants and volunteers can all help here. It is particularly useful to involve students or licensed teachers in training in observation and recording exercises because it will help them practise vitally important skills in looking objectively at what is going on and recording accurately.

Other adults can also help the teacher to gain a clear picture of his own behaviour. Observation of the teacher's response to a child will give information on how often he praises the child, on how often he ignores the child and how often he responds negatively. The teacher will know he is being observed and will therefore modify his behaviour because he is thinking about what he should be doing. That is not to say that he normally behaves differently on purpose but that the knowledge of being observed acts as a reminder of what he thinks he should be doing. Information fed back to the teacher on how he has responded to a given child needs to be sensitively handled for obvious reasons and can be much more useful if the teacher is the person who requests the observations in the first place. It can be even more useful if the teacher is involved in agreeing the areas to be observed.

Children also respond differently to being observed when they know it is happening. It can have a positive or a negative effect on their behaviour, which needs to be taken into account when interpreting results and drawing conclusions. It is curious to note that unacceptable behaviour sometimes disappears when being observed; it is unlikely to be the act of observing alone which affects the behaviour but the attention given by the adult who is doing the observing to his own behaviour. By thinking carefully about the child and what he is doing, the adult concentrates more easily on what he is doing himself.

Incident sheets are a useful way of focusing on what exactly is happening. A record must be kept of serious or unusual incidents of behaviour exhibited, and the way that record is kept will offer much information on which to base a management programme. The form itself (see diagram 3) acts as the reminder of what to observe or at least to note after the event. The incident sheet gives pointers towards the triggers which started the behaviour and begins the process of identifying the reinforcing agent, that is, the thing or things which cause the behaviour to be repeated. The sheet asks for the following information:

What was happening before the behaviour occurred? For example, who was there, and what were they doing? Did anyone hurt or upset the child? Was he stopped from doing something that he wanted to do? These events are called the antecedents. The antecedents are sometimes called 'trigger events'.

A factual description of the behaviour. That is, a precise statement of what the child did.

The consequences of the child's behaviour, that is, the positive or negative things that occurred as a result of or immediately after the behaviour. How did the adult behave in response to the behaviour? This may be pleasant or unpleasant for the child.

Every incident sheet should also be numbered to form part of a school log of incidents (see diagram 4).

Some incident sheets also ask for information on the background or setting in which the behaviour occurs. For example, did the child show the behaviour in the classroom, the playground or in the hall? After a period of similar observations, it may be possible to start to draw conclusions, such as, the child always displays the unacceptable behaviour at a particular time or in a certain place.

A description of what happens after the incident will highlight information on how adults behave with children after problems have occurred, how long it takes the child to calm down and get over the problem, and the results of the adult's intervention, and will indicate whether that intervention proved successful or unsuccessful as a management technique.

The Elton Committee recommended that every school should keep a central record of serious incidents, and should inform the LEA of incidents of serious violent behaviour. Any report that is entered in the school accident book should be reported to the LEA immediately.

The incident log book shows a great deal of information over a period of time, such as how many incidents have occurred; who was involved; which staff were involved; seriousness of incidents. The incident sheets

Diagram 3

INCIDENT SHEET	
NAME OF CHILD _____	DATE OF INCIDENT _____
NAME OF ADULT _____	TIME OF INCIDENT _____

What happened before? A	
Describe the incident – what exactly happened? B	
What happened after the incident? Was anyone hurt?* C	

* If someone was hurt, you must
    a) See to any injuries.
    b) Notify the senior member of staff on duty.
    c) Fill in the accident book.
    d) Copy this sheet to the school nurse.

Incident Book, Log Number:

should be retained and cross-referenced. The Head should sign the book regularly to keep an over-view. The book should be made available to governors with a report on the overall behaviour of children in the school.

Incident sheets, and frequency and duration recording are essential tools, which provide the information necessary to focus clearly on problems. Often teachers will be so closely involved in what is going on that they 'cannot see the wood for the trees'. This is particularly true when the child is displaying serious or extreme behaviours because, as we have seen, such behaviour causes the adult stress and anxiety. There can be a tendency to expect the child to behave in a certain way because of the feeling that he 'always does'. The problem of the self-fulfilling prophecy can be very real in classrooms where there are a number of behaviour problems.

Diagram 4

EXTRACT FROM INCIDENT LOG BOOK					
Name of child	Name of staff	No	Incident	Reported to	Accident Book
S. Brown	P. Smith	8 2.7	Broke window with fist – cuts to arm – hospital treatment.	Head TJ	Yes Parents informed
D. Clarke	P. Smith	9 3rd July	Threw chair – missed adult	Deputy Head TJ	N/A
P. Wills	R. Lyon	10 3rd July	Bit adult's hand – broke skin – hospital for tetanus	Head Teacher TJ	Yes
D. Clarke	R. Hard	11 5th July	Ran away – brought back by police after 2 hours	Head TJ	N/A Parents informed

David

David was known to steal money from coat pockets during break. Because he had been caught on a number of occasions, the natural assumption when money went missing was that David had stolen it. The most extreme example of David's being accused because he was a 'known thief' occurred when he was not even in school. His stated view was that he might as well steal money because he would get blamed anyway. An accurate record of the number of times that money went missing, which included a record of where he was at the time and the likelihood of his being the culprit, showed that on some occasions it could not possibly have been him. This programme was negotiated with David, and, because he knew that the record was being kept and because he had a vested interest in proving that he was not the culprit, he stopped stealing from coat pockets. Money continued to go missing from time to time, but we could prove that it was not David.

A lack of clear records leads to the adult's forgetting the range or seriousness of the problems displayed by a child.

Analysing behaviour

Having observed and recorded behaviour accurately it is necessary to clarify exactly what is happening and to make sure that all adults involved are sharing the same understanding and perception of the problem.

Chapter 2 outlined a commonly used approach to writing clear and precise statements of behaviour, first described by R.F. Mager in 1974, when he suggested that many descriptions of behaviour were 'fuzzies'. He went on to suggest that in order to use descriptions of behaviour positively it was necessary to write them in 'performance' terms that could be clearly observed and measured.

The 'Hey, Dad' test is an easily applied way of examining statements to see if they are fuzzy or clear statements of performance. Simply, if a description of a piece of behaviour can be 'seen', it will pass the test. Add these words to the description of the behaviour, 'Hey, Dad, come and see me ...' If Dad can see exactly what the child is doing, it will be a performance. If Dad has any difficulty in seeing what is happening it will be a 'fuzzy'.

Are the following descriptions 'fuzzies' or 'performances'?

1 Peter is aggressive.
2 He eats with his fingers instead of a knife and fork.
3 She understands the difference between right and wrong.
4 Susan is always messing about in class.
5 George shouts out when asked a question.
6 John tears paper from books.
7 He is the ring-leader when there is any trouble.
8 She hits herself and bites her wrists when frustrated.

The most useful descriptions are the performances, numbers 2, 5, 6 and 8. All those statements will pass the 'Hey, Dad' test because they are observable and not open to subjective interpretation. The other four statements are fuzzy. How could Dad see Peter being aggressive? He might see him hit or scratch someone and be able to share that information clearly with another person; but he could only have a vague idea of what Peter does from the word 'aggressive'. Understanding the difference between right and wrong could relate to murder on the one extreme or to talking in class on the other. This sort of 'fuzzy' is so generalised that it becomes meaningless. 'Messing around in class' or 'being the ring-leader' probably means little to anyone other than the person making the statement. Even that person may have difficulty in remembering the exact behaviour some months later.

Having described the behaviour causing concern in clear and unambiguous statements, it is necessary to prioritise behaviours into those that are the most frequent, last the longest or are the most serious. A general confusion and frustration with a child's behaviours can then be broken down into manageable and understandable smaller behaviours. It is useful to gather this information on to a chart, such as the one that follows, so that it can be analysed or examined carefully.

PRIORITY BEHAVIOUR CHART

NAME _____

List the behaviours causing concern. Be clear.
1
2
3
4
5
6
7
8
9

List the behaviours which cause the most concern
1
2
3

List the positive behaviours
1
2
3

The positive behaviours that the child displays need to be included because they keep things in perspective and give clues towards making an intervention strategy.

Three is an arbitrary number for the priority behaviours but it is manageable and, in the case of children who have complex and wide-ranging problems, it would be difficult or impossible to tackle everything at once. Having established three priority behaviours, it is necessary to gather more information about them, for example:

1 When did the problem start?
2 How long does it last?
3 How often does it occur?
4 How do the other children respond to it?
5 Does the behaviour have an effect
  a on the pupil's own work?
  b on the work of other pupils?
  c on the work of the whole class?
  d on the teacher's teaching:

These questions can be answered in a grid form which allows a 'see at a glance' picture of the seriousness of the behaviours. The grid need not be complicated by written descriptions but marked simply with a tick. The completion of this type of chart (see p. 84) will give a great deal of information with which to form a clear picture of what is happening.

The next step in analysing behaviour is to examine what happened before, the trigger or antecedent. The incident sheet has already been described, including a section for recording antecedents. As we have seen, behaviour needs to be examined against the background or setting in which it occurs and consideration needs to be given to what happened immediately before and then what happened as a result of the behaviour, the consequence.

Often it is the problem behaviour itself that is first noted by the busy teacher and therefore it is that behaviour that is responded to, regardless of whether there was a reason. For example, the child who is seen to punch another child is likely to be dealt with immediately because the behaviour had been witnessed. An awareness of the behaviour that occurred before might change the reaction of the adult. For example, if the teacher had seen the second child pull the first child's hair before he punched him, he may well have responded in a different manner. Concentration on the aspects of the ORA procedure will give teachers the necessary skills to collect information on which to make management decisions. The effect that the antecedent has on the behaviour will become increasingly obvious, the more that structured observation can take place.

KEY POINTS

- The ORA procedure involves observing, analysing and recording behaviour.

- Behaviour needs to be recorded clearly, accurately and concisely.

- Records of behaviour must be easily understood by all concerned with working with the child.

- Record-keeping is an integral part of the process of observation and analysis.

NATURE OF PROBLEM BEHAVIOURS CHART			
Behaviour 1	Behaviour 2	Behaviour 3	
			1 WHEN DID IT START?
			this month
			this term
			this year
			more than 12 months ago
			2 HOW LONG DOES IT LAST?
			seconds
			minutes
			all the lesson
			most of day/all the time
			3 WHEN DOES IT OCCUR?
			frequently in a lesson
			occasionally in a lesson
			every day
			weekly
			4 BEHAVIOUR OF THE OTHERS
			ignore the behaviour
			one pupil encourages it
			several pupils encourage it
			pupils discourage it
			5 EFFECT ON WORK
			disrupts other pupils
			disrupts whole class

- The observation of the child's behaviour is the starting point for planning a management programme.

- Frequency, duration and intensity of the behaviour need to be observed and noted.

- Behaviours, once isolated, need to be prioritised in order to be manageable.

- Antecedents and consequences both affect the frequency, duration and intensity of the behaviour.

Part 2

Management strategies

Part 1 has outlined ways of avoiding and preventing behaviour problems by observing, recording and analysing. Part 2 concentrates on the management strategies; it addresses the question of what can be done to change the child's behaviour, once the problems have been identified.

As we have seen in previous chapters, behaviour is learned. In order to change behaviour, to increase the positive and acceptable and to decrease the negative and unacceptable, it is necessary to understand the effects that rewards, praise and sanctions have on the ways children behave. Simplistically, if a behaviour is increasing or being maintained then it is being reinforced. In order to change a child's behaviour it is necessary to change the way it has been responded to in the past. Part 2 will examine in detail:

1 teaching new skills
2 changing antecedents
3 changing the setting or background in which the behaviour occurs
4 changing the consequences, including positive reinforcement, rewards, sanctions and contracts
5 time out
6 isolation
7 physical restraint
8 writing the programme

1 Teaching new skills

Teaching new skills is one of the most powerful behaviour management strategies available because it is what teachers and parents do anyway. Often, behaviour problems are the result of a child's not having the necessary skills to learn from a task or activity. Tools for learning may include attention control, listening and looking, as well as the more obviously recognised reading and writing skills. For children with learning difficulties a concentration on teaching the skills which are tools for learning will be time well spent. A child with a short attention span or poor concentration will quickly get bored or unsettled if the lesson goes on for too long. If he can be taught to extend his concentration on a task and to find something else to do when he has finished, he will be well occupied and not so likely to behave in a disruptive fashion.

The question of whether the learning difficulty or the behaviour problem comes first was examined in chapter 2, with the conclusion that children with behaviour problems have learning difficulties and those children with learning difficulties will often develop behaviour problems. The extent to which this is true will depend on the structure and organisation in which the child is learning new skills. It is well known that children with learning difficulties need to have carefully structured work, broken down into small and easily achievable steps. The teacher's task is to plan the work so that the child succeeds, ensuring that it is sufficiently challenging to be of interest. The importance of careful and structured planning, close attention to preparation and evaluation of the child's performance and learning has been stressed throughout this book. The same attention to detail is necessary when teaching new behaviours as it is when decreasing unwanted behaviours.

In-service courses such as EDY (Education of the developmentally young), organised from the Hestair Adrian Research Centre in Manchester, are designed to teach staff to approach the task of teaching children with learning difficulties in a structured and carefully planned way. Task Analysis is introduced as a way of cutting down teaching tasks into small and easily tackled stages to meet the needs of individual children. The same approach can be used for teaching appropriate behaviours.

Often the result of teaching a new behaviour will lead to the unwanted behaviour being impossible. Thus, teaching competing behaviours is a deliberate management strategy. Teaching a child to use both hands together at a task would prevent him from self-abusing by slapping his face. This approach increases the frequency of a behaviour that is in direct opposition to a problem behaviour by first teaching the skills and then consistently reinforcing them. A more common example of this approach is in a whole-class situation, where children are taught appropriate working patterns, such as sitting at their desks and working quietly, rather than rushing around the room. The act of putting his hand up and waiting for the teacher's attention may well be a competing behaviour to jumping up and rushing to the teacher's table.

KEY POINTS

- Teaching new skills is one of the most powerful management tools.

- Children with learning difficulties may need to be taught 'tools for learning'.

- Teaching competing behaviour will decrease the opportunity for the unacceptable behaviour to be displayed.

2 Changing antecedents

An examination of the events which occur before the behaviour will indicate ways of minimising or avoiding it. The completed incident sheet will give information on the behaviour triggers and records taken of a particular behaviour over a period of time will often suggest patterns. By analysing these patterns it is likely that ideas will emerge on how to change an approach or set of circumstances. If, for example, the record shows that a child responds negatively when his activity is disrupted, it may be possible to give him early warning that he will have to move on to the next activity in, say, five minutes. Generally, it is useful to give warning of any change of activity so that the children can get used to the idea before it happens. This is particularly true for children who cannot yet tell the time or are unable to remember the sequences of events for long.

Clear instructions tell the child exactly what is expected of him and forestall inappropriate behaviour. Identifying a potential problem early and changing an instruction in order to avoid the difficulty will be useful. For example, if the teacher notices that all the coats in the cloakroom are on the floor, he can send one child to pick them up before sending the children to get their coats, and so avoid the disruption that would follow if the whole class tried to find their coats at once. The teacher should always try to demonstrate acceptable behaviour himself and take every opportunity to divert problems by showing the children a more appropriate way to behave. For example, instead of saying, 'Don't tear the pages', the teacher might say, 'Don't tear the pages. Turn them over, like this'. The demonstration of how to behave shows the teacher's expectation. With less able children, the demonstration is perhaps more important to ensure that they understand what is expected.

Making things that children have got to do more pleasant is another way of changing antecedents and so avoiding or minimising problems. The child who refuses to work because he thinks the task is too difficult can have the task presented in a different way so that he feels more likely to succeed. If the teacher knows he will refuse and possibly become disruptive, he would be foolish to present the task in the same way as when it last caused the problem.

Changing antecedents is in direct line with most of the suggestions outlined in part 1 for preventing and avoiding behaviour problems.

KEY POINTS

- Early warning of a change of activity avoids problems.

- Clear instructions tell children exactly what the teacher expects.

- Acceptable behaviour should be demonstrated by adults to show the child how to behave, instead of telling him off after he has behaved inappropriately.

- Making a disliked activity less unpleasant can help the child to become involved.

3 Changing the setting

Unwanted behaviour can be avoided by removing whatever you anticipate will cause problems, from your knowledge of the child or children and their age and ability levels. As we have seen, observation and careful recording of what is happening over a period of time will give information on potential causes for behaviour problems. The removal of temptation will stop predictable problems from occurring. If a child tears magazines and books obsessionally they need to be removed to avoid the problem. That would, however, only avoid the problem and not teach the child an alternative, more appropriate use of the magazines. The behaviour programme would include structuring a use of books, when the adult could make sure that they were not torn. Efforts would be made to demonstrate how to turn pages and look at pictures, and to teach the child to enjoy magazines. As the child demonstrated a more appropriate use of books and magazines, he could gradually have more time without such close supervision.

Teachers are very experienced at changing the setting in which behaviour problems occur as part of their everyday work. All teachers will have changed the position of children from time to time to avoid spitefulness, unnecessary talking or disruptive behaviour, such as grabbing books or taking pencils. Re-arranging the environment is one way for the adult to take positive action to prevent the child or children from having the opportunity to misbehave. In extreme situations the teacher may use furniture to stop a child from obsessionally running around the classroom, or remove all items that could be thrown before a particular child comes into the classroom. Attention to changing the environment is important in the management of difficult behaviour.

KEY POINTS

- Observation may show the most likely setting for the behaviour and therefore give indications for changing that setting.

- Removing temptation prevents unnecessary confrontation.

- Re-arranging the environment can prevent potential problems.

- Attention to the setting or context within which the behaviour occurs will point to possible changes that can be made.

4 Changing the consequences

Behaviour is more likely to recur if the consequences of the behaviour are reinforced. Behaviour that does not attract a desirable response is unlikely to be repeated. Rewards and sanctions are both consequences which are commonly used, often deliberately, but sometimes unintentionally, with confusing effects on the child and his behaviour.

Before examining the ways in which rewards and in some cases punishments can be used to change behaviour in a positive way, it is necessary to examine the meaning and use of the words, 'reward', 'punishment' and 'reinforcement' and to put them into a usable context. The words reward and reinforcement are often used by people to mean the same thing, but they are not synonymous; they have very distinct meanings.

A reward is a reinforcer, but a reinforcer is not necessarily a reward. A reinforcer can be defined as an action following a piece of behaviour which results in a change in that behaviour. The change may be perceived to be for the better or for the worse. That is, if the behaviour increases as a result of the reinforcer being applied, the reinforcer could be considered a reward – a pleasant event. If the reinforcer results in a decrease in the behaviour, or even in the behaviour stopping altogether, the reinforcer could be regarded as a punishment – an unpleasant event. The word 'reinforcer' is a neutral word in itself; it does not indicate the direction of the change in behaviour, merely that some change has occurred. To say that attention is a reinforcer does not indicate whether the child's behaviour has improved or deteriorated as a result of that attention.

Positive reinforcement and rewards

A positive reinforcer can be considered as a reward, since its application results in an increase in the behaviour. Generally, positive reinforcers are considered to be 'good things', but care needs to be taken that they are positive to the child. The assumption that having five minutes longer at playtime will be a reward for the class does not take account of the fact that, for some children, playtime can be a time when they are bullied. In this instance, what is a positive reinforcer for some children becomes a punishment for others. This example highlights the need for careful observation and recording of the events that lead to an increase in desirable behaviour. More able children will be able to list the things they find rewarding; less able children may need far closer observation and even situations set up to assess their approach to some rewards. The identification of the positive reinforcer is crucial in the task of changing behaviour.

It may be useful at this stage to relate the use of positive reinforcers to everyday life situations to illustrate that they are being used constantly by and with all of us. Some of the most common rewards in life are considered the most important because they are non-material, for example, social contact, attention, warmth, encouragement, a smile and demonstrations of approval. Not only are these common, but they are also immediate and easy to give. To smile and praise a child when he behaves appropriately will positively reinforce him, if he values that praise.

Material rewards have traditionally attracted criticism because of the confusion between bribing and rewarding. The definition of a bribe is: 'Money or other inducement offered to procure (often illegal or dishonest) action in favour of the giver'. The definition of a reward is: 'That which is given in return for good . . . done or received. To repay.' (*Oxford Illustrated Dictionary, 2nd edition*). The clear difference is that the person who benefits from a bribe is the giver and the person who benefits from the reward is the receiver. Rewards of a material kind are given to children from birth onwards, but usually in an inconsistent and often ineffectual manner. Material rewards could take the form of stars, tokens, awards, privileges, good reports, a favourite toy, an extra turn on the swing, and so on. Material rewards are usually a mark of the teacher's attention or pleasure and should always be accompanied by praise and a note of approval, a natural process in most situations. For example, during the traditional prize day the Head will award the certificate or trophy and shake hands with the recipient. Along with the trophy will go a word or two of praise and congratulations.

With young and less able children it may well be necessary to teach an appreciation and enjoyment of non-material rewards through the pairing of praise with something the child really likes. This has been done very successfully with children who do not obviously seem to like physical contact or verbal praise.

Rebecca

Rebecca was making very little progress in any area of school work. She was eight, non-verbal, and she rarely sat still for more than a few moments. She did not like being touched and showed no enjoyment when she was sung to or when her teacher gave her any individual attention. Both her teacher and her parents were concerned that she was becoming more withdrawn as time passed. Over a two-week period, the parents and teachers wrote down everything that Rebecca did that she seemed to enjoy. Enjoyment was measured by Rebecca's smiling or laughing as she was engaged in an activity. The list was not very long but it included her bath, listening to a music-box, milk, and an old stuffed toy. It was decided to work through these, particularly the toy and the music-box, to teach Rebecca to tolerate and then enjoy being spoken to and then being touched. Whenever Rebecca played with the toy or listened to the music-box her teacher would talk with her. Then, the teacher would talk to Rebecca and expect her to stay sitting and reward her with the toy. The same approach was followed at home. Gradually, Rebecca began to show more interest in her teacher and, in time, learnt to enjoy a wider range of attention and activities.

This extreme example has been included deliberately to illustrate that, however difficult it may be to find rewards that a child can enjoy, it is possible with careful observation and thought to find a starting point for all children. Once that point has been found, the reward can be used as the positive reinforcer for other behaviours. Simply, the activity that the child enjoys can be received on condition that the child does something that he enjoys less. In the case of Rebecca, she had to tolerate being spoken to before receiving her favourite toy. With a more able child the reward may be a stated expectation, such as, 'You can do your topic when you have finished your maths.' The topic is used as the positive reinforcer for completing the maths. This is used in a positive way and does not include the use of threats or negative statements to make children achieve.

Positive reinforcers are powerful tools in the management of behaviour because they relate to things that the child enjoys and finds rewarding. It is important to be aware of when and how they work in order to avoid positively reinforcing unacceptable behaviour, for example, in the situation of the child at the till in a supermarket who sees sweets and cries until his mother gives him some. The child has learnt that to cry and throw a temper tantrum will result in his being given the sweets. His temper and crying behaviour is positively reinforced by the sweets and is therefore likely to be the way he tries to get sweets in future. The mother in this example is positively reinforcing unacceptable behaviour by giving in to him. The fact that her response is understand-able does not change the fact that his crying is likely to happen whenever he wants sweets. In this example the behaviour being positively reinforced is the very behaviour that the mother wants to get rid of.

Negative reinforcement

Behaviours can be increased through negative reinforcement. Negative reinforcement can be, simply, the removal of a punishing consequence. For example, a *threat* may be considered a negative reinforcement, if the act of stopping the threat leads to an increase in the behaviour. A teacher may continually threaten the children with punishing consequences if they behave in a particular way. He only stops threatening when they do as he expects. Because they do not want him to start threatening again they continue to behave appropriately. It is not a recommended practice to use threats as a management technique, but the example is a clear illustration of negative reinforcement. Another example might be not punishing a child for owning up to stealing. The child learns to lie instead of telling the truth, if he is punished for owning up to stealing, but by removing the punishment the child is more likely to increase his truth-telling behaviour. The removal of the punishment is the negative reinforcer.

Negative reinforcement of a similar kind is often used to get children to finish a task quickly. Take the common situation where a teacher says to a child, 'You will stay in at playtime until you finish your work.' Assuming the child can do the work set and wants to go out to play, he will be more likely to complete the task quickly to avoid the boredom of staying inside. It is the prospect of boredom and restriction that is the negative reinforcer in this example, made even more powerful if he can see his friends having a good time in the playground.

Negatively reinforced behaviour is very common in everyday life. A child may be involved in an argument every day over the washing-up, but he dislikes the constant nagging from his parents that he does the washing-up to keep them quiet. Negative reinforcement does not always lead to an increase in the desired behaviour, however. Children can often learn an alternative way to avoid the negative consequences. For example, the child threatened with staying in at playtime will soon learn to avoid the consequence by rushing through his work, regardless of quality. It is important, therefore, to use negative reinforcement with a positive reinforcement support so that the child's behaviour is channelled in a more acceptable direction.

Punishment

It is important not to confuse this with punishment, which is an event which follows a behaviour and leads to a decrease in that behaviour. Theoretically, children try to avoid punishing events which are sufficiently undesirable. However, there are a number of problems in using punishments or sanctions as a way of changing behaviour:

1 Punishment teaches only what a child must not do; it does not offer an alternative way to behave.
2 Punished behaviour is likely to re-occur once the punishment or fear of punishment is removed.
3 Repetition of punishment leads to a decrease in its effectiveness as the child gets used to it.
4 Larger and larger doses of punishment need to be administered in order to get the same effect.
5 Punishment can damage adult/child relationships.
6 Punishment teaches that 'might is right'.
7 Punishment leads to avoidance tactics which may be more serious than the original behaviour.

This is not to say that there is no place for sanctions; but careful consideration needs to be paid to the selection and delivery of a punishment, and punishments must be used against a background of positive expectations and reinforcement. Punishment must always be used as a way of teaching the child alternative ways of behaving in the future. It must include the opportunity for the child to see where he has gone wrong and a clear indication of how he is expected to behave the next time. The Elton Report was clear in its findings that schools which put too much emphasis on punishment to deter bad behaviour are likely to be less effective than schools which do not. It is the Committee's opinion, backed up by evidence from a range of groups and institutions, that punitive regimes seem to be associated with worse rather than better behaviour.

In a well-structured, positive working situation the removal or withholding of rewards becomes a powerful 'punisher'. If a child truly values teacher praise and attention, the withholding of it will affect his unacceptable behaviour because of the direct contrast between the lack of response and the more usual positive responses. In a less positive situation, the withholding of attention or praise may be less powerful and not affect the behaviour at all. An expression of disapproval by the teacher may be a positive reinforcer rather than a mild punishment if the child wanted the teacher's attention.

This is not the place to enter the debate on the values and dangers of corporal punishment since corporal punishment has been banned in state schools since the early 1980s. It is illegal to cane, hit or smack a child, and any member of staff caught doing so would be suspended immediately. Schools that have used corporal punishment in the past have had to re-examine their approach to managing pupils who display disruptive behaviour and have had to agree rules of conduct and available sanctions to be used when those rules are infringed. Examples of such 'whole-school policies' will be examined in detail in the next chapter.

For the class teacher the sanctions available for dealing with unacceptable behaviour are limited, which is another reason for developing a positive approach to managing difficult behaviour. Available sanctions might include:

telling off
withholding praise or attention
ignoring
loss of privileges
detention
work during break, eg collecting litter
warning of being sent to senior teacher or Head

Within the school, sanctions might be extended to include:

placement in another class
being 'on report'
being sent to senior teacher or Head.
letter to parents
meeting with parents
suspension
exclusion

Generally the range of sanctions available to teachers and schools is limited, which reinforces the view that punishment alone will not change behaviour. It is rarely acceptable to punish children by stopping them from attending certain lessons or subjects because, under the National Curriculum, all children have an entitlement to the foundation subjects. It is unjustifiable to punish children by giving them extra work in the subject they like least or find hardest; that only serves to make the child associate that subject with punishment, and to increase his chances of failure at it.

Extinction

An extension of the use of withholding praise as a management technique is to decrease an unacceptable behaviour by ignoring it. This will work only if the behaviour is being reinforced by the attention; taking no notice of a behaviour that is being reinforced by something other than attention, such as physical pleasure, will have no effect on the behaviour. Ignoring behaviour that is reinforced by attention is called 'extinction'. As we have seen, the removal of praise in a positive class setting can lead to a decrease in unacceptable behaviour. The logic behind this is that, if the consequences of a behaviour are positively reinforcing that behaviour, the removal of the consequences will result in a decrease of the behaviour. The only danger of ignoring behaviour that is said to be attention-seeking is if the behaviour is being positively reinforced by, for example, peer pressure, or by something other than adult attention. A potentially more serious danger of ignoring behaviour is that it is likely to increase in frequency, duration or intensity.

Interestingly, even if the behaviour is maintained only by adult attention, the act of ignoring the behaviour may lead to an increase in it, at least for a short period of time. This is known as the *'try harder phase'* and quite literally means that the child tries harder to gain the adult's attention by increasing the behaviour. Obviously, this would be an unsuitable technique to use when a child is displaying aggressive or self-destructive behaviour because of the danger of injury.

Extinction will work as a strategy only if everyone is ignoring the same behaviour consistently. It will fail if even one person gives attention to the behaviour because it will then be intermittently reinforced. Research shows that behaviour reinforced in this way is more likely to be maintained because of the 'penny fruit-machine syndrome'. The knowledge that sooner or later the machine will pay out reinforces the gambler to put money in the slot. The gambler also knows that the next time may be the jackpot. Extinction is most useful as a technique when it is matched to a system of positively reinforcing competing behaviours, as we have already seen.

Contracts

Positively reinforcing appropriate behaviour and building on acceptable responses is the most useful approach to managing behaviour problems. The development of a repertoire of positive behaviours will allow the child with behaviour problems to be seen as more acceptable and thus earn positive attention and reinforcement from peers as well as adults. One way to achieve this is by setting up a contract or positive behaviour programme that involves the child and all staff that he comes in contact with. This contract deals with a behaviour or series of behaviours that cause concern and puts the onus on the child to control his behaviour with the support of a written programme. The positive behaviour record below shows a positive behaviour programme designed to focus the child's attention on specified targets.

The expected behaviour was agreed between Robert, his parents, the class teacher and the Head as a result of a series of unacceptable behaviours. He knew that if he could not improve his behaviour he would be suspended from school because his out of class behaviour disrupted the whole school. The chart was originally devised in order to identify the lessons that caused him the most difficulty, to show him and others that his unacceptable behaviour was not happening all the time and to build in the opportunity for him to earn positive reinforcement from adults. This last reason was considered very important because Robert had been disruptive for so long that there was a tendency for adults to blame him for any problems that occurred.

POSITIVE BEHAVIOUR RECORD

NAME   *Robert*

Expected behaviour: Date record started   *6th July*

1 *Robert will stay in the classroom during Lessons.*
2 *Robert will do as he is told by staff.*
3 *Robert will come in when the bell goes.*

Time	MON	TUES	WED	THURS	FRID
9.30–10.00					
10.00–10.30					
10.30–11.00					
11.00–11.30					
11.30–12.00					
12.00–12.30					
12.30–1.00					
1.00–1.30					
1.30–2.00					
2.00–2.30					
2.30–3.00					
3.00–3.30					

√ for behaving as expected
Add initials } eg LS Maths
Add subjects

If behaviour is not as expected put initials and subject only.

The additional attention he received from making the effort to follow the 'rules' resulted in a self-fulfilling prophecy. The better Robert behaved, the more praise and attention he received and the more attention he received the more he tried to behave. The contact with his parents was helpful and supportive to Robert in his efforts to stay on task.

POSITIVE BEHAVIOUR CHART

Name _____

Expected behaviour: Date record started _____

1 _____

2 _____

3 _____

DAY & DATE	MORNING	LUNCH TIME	AFTERNOON
MONDAY 12th June			
TUESDAY 13th June			
WEDNESDAY 14th June			
THURSDAY 15th June			
FRIDAY 16th June			
TOTALS			

Grand total _____ out of 15 possible ticks

√ for behaving as expected – add initials

Leave blank if behaviour is not as expected

Signature of pupil _____

The improvement in his behaviour was so marked by the end of the second week that a different positive behaviour chart (above) was designed, again with his involvement, aiming at longer periods of time when he had to behave in the expected manner. The chart alone became the support, and was gradually phased out as Robert learnt to cope.

The above case study has been included because it illustrates many aspects of the management strategies contained in the section on changing the consequences of the behaviour. Of course, in order to begin the programme it had been essential to gather information about the problems Robert had been displaying and to identify the potential reinforcing agents. In his case the positive attention from his teacher, his parents and the Head were important, but when he was failing consistently, peer pressure took over. He had to succeed in order to gain the positive attention from adults and the very nature of his success removed the positive reinforcement from his peers to his unacceptable behaviour.

Various forms of punishment had been tried before, with little success and although his inappropriate behaviour had largely been for attention it could not be ignored because it was too serious.

KEY POINTS

- A positive reinforcer is an event which follows a piece of behaviour and results in an increase in that behaviour.

- Rewards can be material and non-material but must be positively reinforcing to the child.

- Negative reinforcement is the removal of an unpleasant consequence, resulting in an increase in the behaviour.

- Punishment is an event which follows a behaviour and leads to a decrease in that behaviour.

- Punishment should be considered carefully because it teaches only what not to do.

- Extinction is the removal of the consequences of a behaviour and leads to a decrease in that behaviour.

5 Time out from reinforcement

Technically, time out from reinforcement, or 'time out' as it has become known, is a strategy which involves changing the consequences of a behaviour. It could have been included in the previous section, but it has been given a section in its own right because of the confusion and concern it causes. It is important to clarify exactly what it is and to put it into a reasonable and useful context.

Time out involves moving the child from a reinforcing setting and putting him in a setting where there is no stimulation. It can be interpreted in a similar way to extinction, in that both strategies involve the removal of positive reinforcers. If used as a carefully planned management strategy, 'time out' is not a punishment since it is removing the child, in a calm and non-threatening way, from a situation that he cannot control into a stimulus-free, quiet area where he will receive no attention from other people. If the child were removed in an angry, negative way to a dark or frightening place, it would clearly be a punishment and would be an unacceptable strategy.

Parents and teachers use 'time out' as a punishment when they send a child from the table for misbehaving, or to their room, with the statement, '. . . and you can stay there until you learn how to behave.' It is often a response of desperation because the child's behaviour has become unacceptable. All it does, however, is to give the adults some space and peace. It will not effectively change the child's behaviour. A child put outside a classroom door because he has behaved badly may have been removed from a reinforcing situation but is likely to have been placed in a potentially more reinforcing situation. Everyone who walks past is likely to talk to him; some will tell him off; other children may tease him or congratulate him on his ability to get out of the lesson. If no one is around he may revert to destructive behaviour, tearing wallpaper or displays, or, even worse, run off, causing disruption to others or putting himself at risk by leaving the school site. The behaviour that resulted in his being removed from the classroom has long since been forgotten as the opportunity for further disruption grows.

Removing the child to the Head's office can have little real effect on the child's behaviour. If this move is not part of a planned intervention strategy it can be reinforcing to the child, as there is so much going on in the office part of the school – telephone calls, visitors, parents. It is not unknown for children to behave in an unacceptable fashion because they know that it will result in a period in the Head's room, away from the classroom and work. This is not to say that children should never be taken or sent to the Head for sanctions, but it must be realised that this is the ultimate available to the class teacher and should not be used lightly or too frequently. Occasionally, it has been necessary to arrange for a child to be placed in the Head's office for safety, or to give the teacher space. This is more for the sanity and protection of the teacher than a part of an effective behaviour management strategy. It is none the less extremely important as part of a staff support system.

'Time out' should be used as a strategy only if the following conditions apply:

1 The child would prefer to be in the classroom, or with the group.
2 The room or area that the child is removed to is unstimulating.
3 The child is removed in a calm and non-punishing way.
4 The child is brought out of 'time out' after the time span agreed, usually in under ten minutes.
5 The child is positively welcomed back into the classroom with no further reference to his previous behaviour.
6 The child is supervised at all times during 'time out'.
7 A careful and accurate record is kept.

Few schools have a 'time out' room specifically designed for the purpose, but the same rules and safety standards must apply to any room being used.

It is possible to set up a situation where a child places himself on 'time out'. The opportunity to remove himself from a situation where he cannot cope because other people are reinforcing his unacceptable behaviour is a way of teaching self-control. Care needs to be taken that this does not become an opportunity for the child to opt out of lessons that he is not interested in, but is built into his agreed programme. In one instance, a child who had previously run away from school if things became too difficult for him agreed to take himself to a quiet area until he had calmed down. The checks on this were built into the programme.

1 He had to tell the secretary that he was going to the room.
2 The secretary would inform the class teacher.
3 The class teacher would set a timer to ring after five minutes to tell him to return to the class, because he could not tell the time at this stage.
4 He would return to the class, with a quiet word of praise from the teacher.
5 A record was kept of the number of times he had felt it necessary to go to the quiet room. This was used to show him how well he was coping.

As with all programmes, management programmes involving 'time out' must be carefully monitored to ensure that it is having the desired effect on the behaviour. If the behaviour is not decreasing but being maintained or increasing, then 'time out' may well be the wrong method to use. Attention must be paid to the number of occasions that 'time out' has been used, as part of that monitoring; if the child is spending more time away from the classroom than in it, the method is of little use.

Teachers of very disturbed children find it a problem to get the child to the 'time out' room in the first place, if the child is behaving in a dangerous manner and refuses to move or to walk independently. This raises the issues of isolation and physical restraint.

KEY POINTS

- Time out is the removal of the child from the reinforcer.

- Time out is not a punishment.

- Time out must be used only as a part of a structured individual programme and its use must be fully recorded.

- That record and the programme must be fully monitored to ensure that it is working.

6 Isolation

At times, there is confusion between 'time out' and isolation; the main difference between the two in the context of this book is that 'time out' is used as part of a planned management programme designed to modify the child's behaviour, whereas isolation is used in response to serious and dangerous behaviours, in order to prevent injury to the child or to others.

In extreme situations it may be necessary to isolate a child. Isolation is not suggested as a management technique in its own right because it must be used only as a last resort in order to cope with a dangerous situation. In normal circumstances children must not be isolated from their peers nor placed in a secure situation that they cannot get out of. When working with very disturbed children, however, there may be times when it is necessary to isolate a child for a period of time. Isolation must be used only in the following circumstances:

1 When the child's behaviour is putting him at physical risk.
2 When the child's behaviour is placing other children in danger.
3 When a child's behaviour is causing a member of staff to be physically at risk.
4 When a child's behaviour seriously damages property.

If a 'time out' room or other secure room is ever to be used for isolation there must be a written policy that has been agreed with governors, incorporating tight supervision and procedures. This is to protect the rights of the child and to protect the staff who are isolating the child. It would be advisable to involve parents in the planning stage, if it seemed likely that a child's behaviour was so extreme that he might need isolating. Parents must be informed immediately if their child is isolated as the result of a serious crisis, and a case conference must be convened as soon as it is practical to discuss future strategies.

Isolation is not to be used as a punishment and children must not be threatened with its use. It is important to specify the staff who can authorise a child's being isolated (probably senior staff because of the extreme nature of the behaviour and the response) and to make sure that they all know the procedure to follow.

1 Individual record sheets should be kept (see example sheet below).
2 A central log must be kept to show the number of times children have been isolated, noting the child's name, staff name, length of isolation and the incident(s) which led to the decision.
3 If isolation is in response to a crisis, the Head or deputy must be informed immediately and a formal review held as a matter of urgency.

4 The child must be supervised at all times.
5 The aim should be to calm the child and remove him from isolation as soon as possible. This is the decision of the senior member of staff.
6 When calm, the child must be re-integrated into his group. The senior member of staff decides when this is safe.

It is, of course, essential to involve medical and psychological services, if a school is having severe problems. In most cases when behaviour of this severity is displayed the school will already know that additional resources and support are necessary and will have involved other professionals as a matter of course. It must be stated that incidents of this severity are rare and do not occur at all in the majority of schools. It would be misleading to categorise the types of schools that may expect to manage children who display extreme behaviour problems, because, as we have seen, the severity of the problems relies on a wide range of factors.

Opposite is an example of an individual record sheet which is designed to gather sufficient information to monitor the use of isolation. It is deliberately detailed in order to protect the child and the staff and will provide information on which to build an appropriate intervention programme. The Head countersigns the form to show that it has been read and noted and, as a double check, would be advised to read and sign the central record.

If there is any suggestion that a child will hurt himself when in isolation, physical restraint must be used. Items that could be used as weapons should be removed from the child before he goes into isolation. A doctor's help may be necessary to sedate the child in the most extreme situations.

KEY POINTS

• Isolation must be used only in extreme situations when people are at physical risk.

• Exceptionally, it may be necessary to prevent serious damage to property.

• There must be a written policy and procedure on the use of isolation.

• A full record must be kept.

• Medical and psychological services may need to be involved.

• Parents must always be involved in decision-making and planning.

7 Physical restraint

Physical restraint is an immediate method of stopping someone from hurting himself or another person. Physical restraint needs to be used

INDIVIDUAL RECORD SHEET – ISOLATION

To be completed and given to the Head EVERY time the child is isolated

Name of child.................................... Date..

Name of staff.................................... Entry time..............................

Exit time ....

Authorising member of senior staff..

1 Description of incident leading to decision to isolate child.
   [Include staff/pupil names and attach incident sheet.]

2 Observation of child's behaviour whilst in isolation.
   [Continue on a separate sheet, if necessary.]

3 What happened afterwards? [Re-integration process.]

Central record book must   Staff signature...............................
be completed.
                                  Head teacher.................................

---

in a way that calms the child and does not frighten or hurt him. As with isolation and 'time out' it is not a punishment. No restraint is permissible in school other than physical restraint using the adult's body to control the child's body. In physical restraint, force can be increased or relaxed in direct ratio to the resistance offered by the child.

Physical restraint is usually thought of in relation to extreme and usually aggressive incidents but is used in a far wider set of circumstances. For example, holding a child's hand when out could be a form of physical restraint if the result of letting go would be that the child would run out into the road. Holding the hand of a child who hits himself is another form of physical restraint with self-abusive children. Many children respond positively to the application of gentle restraint because it can provide a sense of security and allows the child a way out of a problem. A hand on a child's arm could be enough of a physical gesture to prevent him from hitting another child.

When managing children who behave in a physically aggressive or violent manner, a number of points need to be borne in mind in order to avoid or minimise the need for physical restraint.

1 It is not always possible to avoid children's aggressive and violent acts but efforts must be made to calm the situation rather than make it worse.
2 Physical or verbal aggression from an adult does not relieve the problem – it is likely to result in more serious aggression from the child.
3 Adults need to respond in a calm and clear manner.
4 Remove the other children from the situation. Call or send for assistance.
5 Approach the child and, if he is responsive, try to talk him down.
6 Avoid reacting to abusive remarks and do not enter into an argument.
7 Do not attempt to restrain the child alone unless you are confident that you can cope. Be aware that the amount of physical force required could result in injury to the child or to you.
8 Make every effort to avoid physical contact until help is available; but, if waiting would result in an increased risk of violence you could not wait.
9 Attempt to remove any object that could be used as a weapon.

The same rules apply to physical restraint as apply to isolation: it should be used only when there is danger of the child's hurting himself, another child or an adult. As a general rule, a second member of staff should be on hand when physical restraint is necessary, to offer support and to act as a witness, if necessary.

1 Restraint should be applied in a manner which attempts to calm rather than provoke aggressive responses from the child.
2 The degree of force used should be the minimum required to control the danger.
3 Clothing, rather than limbs, should be used whenever possible to control dangerous movements.
4 Restrain by holding the child's clothing at the top of his arms. This

can become a bear hug if necessary. (Beware head butting if restraining from behind; kicking if restraining from in front.)

5 The sooner the child can face the adult the better, as it is less likely to be frightening.

6 In some extreme cases the child will need to be restrained on the floor. This will take two people.

7 The child should be moved to a quieter environment as soon as he is calmer.

In all difficult behaviour management situations and particularly when physical restraint is necessary, the dignity of the child should be respected at all times. The child has a right to be told why the behaviour displayed is unacceptable, but in a calming and reassuring manner. Counselling should be offered after the event, to give the child the opportunity to talk through what happened and make amends. It is important, too, to respect the dignity of staff, who may feel uncomfortable, embarrassed or even frightened at having to restrain a child. Positive support is essential after the event as well as during the incident for both child and adult(s).

All serious incidents of aggression or violence need to be reported to the Head or a senior member of staff, who will take any action that is then necessary. If the child is hurt during the restraint process, medical attention must be sought immediately and a full report submitted to the Head, who will inform the parents. It is well known with some extreme behaviour problems that there is an increased risk of the child or adult getting hurt, which is one of the most important reasons for close communication with parents, a clear and agreed procedure to follow and a structured and immediate recording system.

KEY POINTS

• Physical restraint should be used only to stop a child from hurting himself, another child or an adult.

• It is vital to try to calm the child during restraint. Efforts must be made to avoid hurting or frightening the child.

• A record of serious incidents of aggression and the use of restraint must be kept. Parents must be fully informed.

8 Writing the programme

When all the options have been considered and the decisions made, it is necessary to write down the programme of behavioural support. This is a vital aspect of the procedure as the structure of the programme report will act as a checklist to ensure that consideration has been given to all aspects. The programme must be concisely written to ensure that it is easy for all the staff to understand and follow.

The written programme should have sections on the following:

1 An indication of consultation undertaken and those involved. (Was it a formal review meeting? Are the parents aware?)
2 Agreement on the priority needs – hierarchical order.
3 Specific difficulties staff are likely to encounter – to enable staff to anticipate the style and level of response of the pupil.
4 Specific strengths and interests of the pupil – to provide all staff with some tools for competing behaviour, prevention of crisis, etc.
5 Resources to be made available for the programme – it may be rooms, physical resources, or the availability of staff time or guidance.
6 Identification of the key member of staff leading the programme – normally the class teacher.
7 Curriculum issues – details of any changes in timetable, support staff, withdrawal, etc, with detailed times.
8 The agreed behavioural programme – what it is specifically, and how it is implemented consistently. The programme will impinge on all other items on this list but issues for consideration are:
   – activities building on present strengths.
   – teaching the pupil self-development strategies.
   – diagnostic checklists for observation work in classes or around the school.
   – statement of specific objectives for the programme.
   – clear time scale.
   – any modification required to work levels/pressures during the programme.
   – additional resources available for the pupil during the programme.
   – clear statement of style of response and discussion with the pupil during the programme.
   – clear statement on acceptance of levels of interaction between pupils and peers during programme (and indication of adult intervention).
   – changes required to class or school security arrangements.
   – monitoring arrangements for the programme.
   – distribution list for the programme.
   – review/observation/record sheets should be attached.
   – awareness of parents and any other professionals and their involvement in the programme.
   – procedure for staff to modify the programme during its course and inform others of any changes.
   – date by which pupil will be fully informed of the programme and programme starting date.
   – date of next review on pupil.

SUMMARY: TEN-POINT PLAN

1 Observe the behaviour(s).
2 Analyse the behaviour(s)—isolate and identify the problem clearly.
3 Record information about the behaviour(s):
    intensity—frequency—duration
  then make a priority list of target behaviours.
  Record the ABC:
    antecedents—behaviour/background—consequences.
4 Isolate the 'triggers'.
5 Identify the reinforcers.
6 Compare notes to ensure everyone perceives the problem in the same way.
7 Decide on management strategies.
8 Write the programme.
9 Implement the programme.
10 Monitor its effectiveness and modify accordingly.

4

A whole-school approach

Introduction

The Elton Report clearly referred to the responsibility of all staff to share in the development of school processes and procedures in order to influence substantially children's behaviour so that effective teaching and learning can take place. Improvements in general standards of behaviour can be brought about through institutional change made possible by in-school evaluation and review. The more involved staff, parents and, where possible, children are in that process, the more valued each will feel. The school will take on a positive direction with shared aims and clearly stated objectives.

Teachers will often describe their greatest concern as being the lack of time available for each child because of the demands of an individual child or small group who have additional needs. The range of organisational and planning skills described in this chapter are designed to illustrate the need for teachers to work as part of a team, to contribute to professional discussions and to evaluate not only classroom teaching but also their role within the school. Every adult who works in the school has a responsibility for the children and for the education they receive, but some have additional specific roles and responsibilities.

Much has been written about the role of the Head and numerous papers have described management styles and suggested different approaches that may work according to the situation, the stage of the school's development and so on. The common theme is that the Head plays a vital key role in the overall effectiveness of the school. In behaviour management, the Head's role is central to the establishment of whole-school approaches to staff development, staff management and staff support. Without effective approaches and policies there is a very real danger of individuals working in isolation, children failing, a lack of direction as well as low morale, with both staff and children feeling demoralised and under-valued.

This chapter examines some of the whole-school approaches that are essential in supporting children with behaviour problems and enabling staff and parents to work together to ensure the highest possible standards of behaviour and learning for children.

1 *The starting point*

Once the school accepts the principle that the expertise to deal with children and young people with additional behaviour problems largely lies in the hands of staff and parents, it will need to establish a starting point, which must be a statement of where the school is now, what is working well, what areas need attention and how that attention is to be given. One way to do this is to establish a draft series of concise, clear and relevant policies for crisis management and day-to-day working, in order to encourage a collective responsibility. The range of policies should include the following:

- Clear management structure for all areas of the school
- Rewards, praise and sanctions
- Working with parents
- Guidelines for compiling strategies for managing children
- Reporting and record-keeping system
- Staff support and development system
- Reviews on individual children
- Communication systems
- INSET

These whole-school policies are in the specific area of behavioural support, and are additional to other key whole-school policies, each of which should take into account the needs of pupils with behaviour problems. Other central areas are:

- Curriculum
- Pastoral care
- Special educational needs
- Personal, social and moral education
- Assessment, marking and work presentation
- Study skills
- Links with parents

It is of value to consider the entitlement of the individual student within the whole-school policy. The diagram below indicates the rights of the individual, whatever his learning or behavioural problem, within the school system. If such an entitlement model is accepted, there are serious implications for the organisation and support methods used in many schools. There is a clear 'resource' implication within any school to ensure access to 'specialist' staff and, if necessary, support staff. The

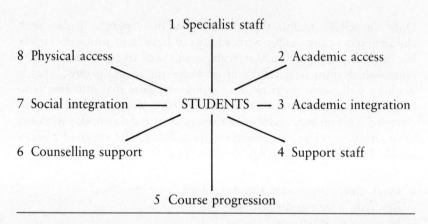

WHOLE-SCHOOL POLICY

1 Specialist staff

8 Physical access   2 Academic access

7 Social integration —— STUDENTS — 3 Academic integration

6 Counselling support   4 Support staff

5 Course progression

model does not presume that the specialist and support staff come from outside the school.

Each school will be at a *different stage of development* in these areas, and for this reason no attempt has been made to list the areas in terms of priority. That is for each school to do in relation to its perceived need at any given time. There may well be other areas that could be included, essential to the development of a whole-school approach to meeting the needs of children with additional behaviour problems, but if the above are all agreed and implemented a sound base will be in place.

As part of the implementation process, schools need to ensure that all interested parties have had an opportunity to contribute, for example, governors, parents and other professionals, as necessary. If the policies have been drawn up by the staff group or, in a large school, their representatives, there will be a sense of ownership and responsibility. The more an individual feels he has been involved in the planning stage, the more committed he will be to the implementation. In some cases, it will be useful to involve the pupils in some aspects of this planning – after all the school is there to meet their needs – but this may not always be appropriate.

It is important to write draft policies for some of the above areas because, quite simply, until they have been implemented it would be difficult to tell if they were right for the school. The very nature of a school is that it is continually changing to meet the needs of the children, the expectations of parents, the community, the LEA and the government. There needs to be a system for monitoring the policies, with opportunities for people to feed back and contribute to any modifications that may be necessary.

2 *Sharing responsibility*

The underlying philosophy in a school where there are children with learning difficulties and additional behaviour problems must be upon expecting and demanding high standards of behaviour and showing that, when effort has been made, it is valued. There must be a move away from a regime which focuses on sanctions and punishments and constantly draws attention to the pupils' misdemeanours and mistakes.

The commitment to meeting the individual as well as group needs of the children and young people must be shared by all staff who come into contact with them. This will include domestic staff, child care staff, classroom assistants, coach guides, speech therapists and physiotherapists, as well as teachers. All have a right to and need for in-service training in the individual and group needs of the children, levels of acceptable behaviour, appropriate adult responses, as well as management strategies. Intrinsic to this would be the shared knowledge and acceptance that working with children who have additional behaviour problems demands tolerance and patience, and the opportunity to gain deeper understanding of individual needs.

Sharing responsibility would be impossible without working with parents and those taking on the parental role, such as child care workers, both in the residential school setting and in the hostel or children's home. The move towards fostering for young people with learning difficulties and additional behaviour problems increases the group of people who need to be involved in discussions and joint planning for meeting the needs of the whole child twenty-four hours a day. Clearly, consistent management is easier when fewer people are involved, but clear, well-publicised and consistently applied rules and expectations can be established for both individuals and schools. The emphasis is upon a shared target for standards of behaviour and consistent responses to breaches of that behaviour. Policies should be realistic, should specify rules and responsibilities and indicate who to go to for support and extra guidance.

The sections that follow examine the issues relating to each area of school policy as listed above. The summary of each section will include a sample whole-school policy relating to that area. It may have been written specifically for a special or a mainstream school, but should serve to illustrate the range of issues that need to be examined.

3 Management structure for the school

Effective management and organisation of a school can enable both parents and staff to feel valued, confident and part of a team committed to meeting the needs of all children. A clear and well communicated management structure will ensure that all members of staff know who to go to for what, who is responsible for each area of the school and where the lines of accountability are.

Each member of staff will need a carefully planned and negotiated job description, which is then shared with all staff. Some aspects of this will be the same from one teacher to the next, as agreed in *Teachers' Pay and Conditions (1986)*, but other aspects will vary according to the children and subjects taught. It is as important to share the job description and areas of responsibility of the Head and deputy as any other member of staff's. Careful consideration needs to be given to responsibility for meeting the needs of children with special difficulties, and this responsibility will need to be included in all job descriptions in some form or another, to reflect the wide range of behaviour problems and learning difficulties in schools today.

The management structure of the school will also cover management of the curriculum and therefore indicate which member of staff is responsible for core areas, for co-ordination of assessment and testing and for monitoring individual programmes. A carefully planned structure will ensure that, even in a small school, each aspect of the child's education is being monitored by a specified person, who is responsible to a named senior person. Clarification of areas of responsibility is a support to the class teacher; and it allows the Head to delegate clear responsibilities in a structure that is easily monitored and reviewed (see Chapter 6). By devolving responsibilities throughout the staff there is more likelihood of a quality service being developed, given that senior staff continue to monitor closely what is going on.

In a behavioural emergency, staff need to be able to contact a named person. Such a system of contact will vary according to the potential emergency and to the particular class or child. Consideration needs to be made of issues such as the location of a particular group of children in relation to, for example, senior staff; the cover arrangements for break time, particularly in wet weather; and procedures for children arriving at and leaving school. Clear procedures need to be established for taking children off site, in terms of where they can go and what additional supervision is necessary to ensure safety; staff must feel confident, not only in their ability to manage individuals but also in the organised procedure in the case of an emergency, for example, if a child gets lost, has an accident or a major aggressive outburst. There should be statements covering the maximum number of children to go off site with a teacher at a time, how many children a classroom assistant can take out and appropriate places to take children at particular times. The establishment of a set of clear procedures will provide a useful support network for staff, parents and children alike.

All staff need to know who is 'on duty' and the responsibilities of that particular role. The child who is causing concern will have a great deal of attention focused upon him; such attention will need to be channelled into a whole-school management strategy in order to support him positively and to enable staff to know what to do in the case of a serious outburst.

The most obvious example of such a strategy is when taking out in public a child who is known to have aggressive or violent outbursts. Forward planning and careful attention will be needed to ensure that staff know what to do, should a violent outburst occur. In such an extreme situation those staff who are not in daily contact with the child will need as much information on what to do in an emergency as those who know the child well. This is because extreme situations undoubtedly cause varying degrees of anxiety in people who are on the periphery as well as in those who are handling the situation.

Serious incidents in public – steps to follow

Before you leave

1 Get permission from a senior member of staff to take the child out.
2 State where you are going and approximately when you will be back.
3 Check child's behaviour programme for:
  agreed restraint procedure
  known 'triggers', eg fear of dogs.
4 Make sure there are at least two members of staff.
5 Make sure at least one knows the child/children.
6 Agree areas of responsibility before setting off; who is supervising which child, who is in charge, etc.
7 Take the school phone number and money for a call.
8 If concerned about ability to manage the child/group, don't go. Safety is most important.

When out

1 Tight supervision is essential.
2 Never leave children unattended.
3 Don't take unnecessary risks, eg, stay away from over-crowded areas.

4 Identify problems early. Return to school or phone for help before the incident gets out of hand, if possible.
5 Should an incident occur, make sure the other children are safe and well supervised.
6 Ask a member of the public to phone for help to
   i school
   ii the police, if very serious or if far from school.
7 Follow restraint procedure – attempt to calm the child.
8 After the incident, explain what has occurred to any passers-by; take the address of any member of the public who is concerned.
9 Return to school as soon as possible.

When you return

1 Inform senior member of staff on duty.
2 Complete incident sheet.
3 Discuss incident with senior colleague.
   – Could it have been avoided?
   – What should be done next time?
   – How can other staff be informed, calmly?
   – Are the other children all right?
   – Were they frightened by the incident?
   – Did they make it worse?
4 Senior member of staff to inform parents.

In most cases it will be the Head or deputy who informs parents of a serious incident to their child. The Head needs to inform at least the Chairperson of Governors when any serious incident occurs and should keep the Chair informed of concerns raised about individual children who have behaviour problems. As in all aspects of this chapter, it is necessary to have a whole-school statement on these issues and for the Head to make sure that all staff have access to that statement.

Because there is a far greater chance of children with behaviour problems having accidents, it is worth providing an example of a procedure to be followed, should someone be hurt. The accident may be to the child who is severely disturbed, to another child, staff member or member of the public.

Accident procedure

All staff must make sure they are familiar with the first aid information on the wall in the staff room. Another child can be sent for help, or in class 3, the buzzer can be used to summon help in an emergency. When off site, always carry the school telephone number and a ten-pence piece; in a serious situation a member of the public can be asked to get help for you while you stay with the child.

1 Stay calm and get help immediately.
2 Do not attempt to move the child/adult.
3 If the accident looks serious, a member of staff (or a member of the public, if off site) will phone for an ambulance.
4 Make sure the other children are moved to a place of safety.
5 Stay with the child until medical help arrives.
6 Give a clear and factual report of what has happened.

After attending to first aid, or ensuring the appropriate medical treatment has been made available, YOU NEED TO

1 Make sure that the Head is fully aware of what has happened.
2 Write an incident sheet including subsequent medical treatment.
3 Give copies of the completed incident sheet to the Head, school nurse, class teacher and the child's file. (This information forms the basis of not only programme planning for the child, but any report the Head may have to make to parents or governors. It is therefore essential that the sheet is completed fully.)
3 Complete the accident book.
4 Complete and sign the Health and Safety accident form.

The procedures that need to be followed in the case of a behavioural emergency or accident must be clearly stated, so that the member of staff knows what to do and can check the list to make sure that all the right people have been informed and that the necessary paperwork has been completed.

4 *Rewards, praise and sanctions*

Major issues, such as the school's overall aims, the desirability and relevance of rewards, rules and sanctions should be open to discussion by interested members of staff and decisions should be taken, where possible, in relation to the needs of individuals as well as to the needs of the school as a whole.

Consistency between staff is crucial to the success of the whole-school approach. It is only too clear what happens when, for example, a 'strong' teacher releases a class of children to a 'weak' teacher; the children misbehave. If the strong teacher has reached the level of discipline by, at worst, threatening the children or frightening them into complying, he will be undermining the work of his less dominant colleagues. The children will respond differently in the two settings in terms of behaviour but will not necessarily learn more effectively with the teacher who uses extreme measures to control. An individual child needs consistent behaviour management in order to respond positively. It is of little use overall for one member of staff to be able to manage and support a child if that control cannot be transferred into other settings with different people. A way of balancing different approaches into a consistent approach which uses the best of each is desirable. The children will know what is expected of them and what will happen if they do not comply, without having to suffer a negative and punitive regime.

As we have seen in relation to rules in the classroom, whole-school rules should be few in number and sensible in their implementation. They must be seen to be fair, both to children and staff, allowing equal opportunity for all to succeed, and they must change and develop in response to the changing needs of the children. In general, such rules will rely on an expectation that children and adults alike will treat each other with respect, making every effort to behave in a way that does not hurt, disrupt or irritate other people. Adults need to listen to what children are saying and demonstrate that they understand and care for them. Emphasis must be placed upon a positive and encouraging response to the children through effective classroom teaching and child care practice.

The development of the school approach and policy towards a consistent use of rewards, praise and sanctions will link closely to the overall expectations of the children and the aims of the school as a whole. If the school is intent on setting high standards in all activities and demanding outstanding work at all times, it will need to establish a consistent approach to showing children that their efforts are valued. This will involve encouragement and praise, in formal and informal situations, for effort as well as achievement; a recognition that all children, with the right support can make progress; and the acknowledgement by a structured system of rewards of that progress and effort. Different schools respond in different ways to the question of rewards. Some have a system of house points, good marks or other tokens which stand for a statement of the child's achievement. Others rely more heavily on verbal praise and encouragement. A mixture of both would be ideal, where children could show a physical token of the adult's positive attention. This is particularly important for the very young child or the child who has limited language ability. The physical token, be it a smiling face, a star on a piece of work or a special badge, can be easily recognised by all adults and reinforced continuously. The child will have something to take home and share with his parents.

As always, the issue of age appropriateness is crucial when looking at a reward system for older children. Secondary pupils who have learning difficulties are extremely sensitive to their own problems and, understandably, react badly to being patronised or treated as if they were young children. Unfortunately, the less able the young person, the more likely it is that adults will respond as if he were very young, even talking about him as if he did not understand. Any school approach to rewards must take account of the feelings and needs of the age group of children in the school and, as with all teaching programmes, must show progression that reflects the pupil's growing maturity. Tokens for sixteen year-olds would be unacceptable and insulting.

When sanctions are used against a background of high expectations, positive reinforcement for efforts made and clear indications that each child is a valued member of the school, no matter what his particular problems, there is a chance of their being meaningful. When a child knows what is expected of him and understands why he needs to behave in an appropriate way, he is able to share the values of the school. The more involved the children are in the establishment of the school system for rewards, expectations and sanctions, the more likely they will be to try to follow them. Some children may be unable to contribute fully to a discussion, either because they have limited language skills or because their behaviour is so disturbed that they need a management support programme implemented for them, but under-expectation of the child's potential ability to contribute should be avoided.

One of the most useful and immediate sanctions available is disapproval from a respected adult. The consistent approach to high expectations and the organised use of rewards will support those teachers who have difficulty in managing children with additional behaviour problems because it will provide a shared framework for working. The fact that everyone is working in the same general direction with similar expectations will avoid confusion for the child and fewer opportunities for manipulation between one adult and another. Joint working minimises the opportunities for children to 'play off' one adult against another.

The staff need to agree a list of sanctions in the same way as they agree the system of rewards. They need to state the conditions in which sanctions will be imposed, and to indicate how to ensure the child understands what he has done and how he can avoid making the same mistake in future. Sanctions must never work against the principles of the school. For example, punishing a child for not working by giving him more work to do is more likely to alienate the child from the learning situation than to provide an opportunity for him to succeed next time. The example below of one school's policy on rewards and sanctions gives an idea of the range available to a teacher or a school.

Rewards and sanctions – a primary school policy

Greatest emphasis must be placed upon praise and reward for effort and achievement. Good discipline is a high priority. Schools rules and the consequences of breaking them are shared openly with parents and pupils. The school works positively with parents in order to form an open and trusting relationship, so that areas of difficulty are noted and acted upon early.

All staff share the responsibility for ensuring good behaviour in the classroom and elsewhere. Good behaviour will be achieved if staff recognise children's difficulties and work together to overcome them, and acknowledge and reward their strengths.

Rewards

1 All work will be marked regularly.
2 Special effort or achievement will be rewarded with a star. Three stars will be entered as a credit mark on the chart in the front hall.
3 Credit marks will be announced in assembly and, where appropriate, the piece of work will be shown.
4 Parents are to be informed through the homework book if their child has been awarded a credit mark.
5 Children's work must be displayed as often as possible. It must be presented to a high standard and clearly marked with the child's name and the date the work was completed.
6 Children should be encouraged to take work to the Head or deputy when they have made a special effort.
7 The Head will write home to parents to report on any particular achievement.

Note Individual children may need specific programmes rewarding appropriate behaviour from time to time. These would be in addition to the general expectation that children are encouraged and praised at every opportunity.

Sanctions

1 Withdrawal of privileges, eg, outings, lunchtime clubs, youth club, etc.
2 Full report – relating to behaviour and work, to be completed at the end of each lesson.
3 Full report – as above, but to be taken to the Head at the end of the day/week.

4 Detention – at break time.
   (*Note* Putting the whole class on detention for the misdemeanours of one or two children will cause resentment.
5 Detention – after school.
   (*Note* Parents must be given 24 hours' notice of detention.)
6 Letter to parents, leading to meeting with parents, Head and child.
7 Suspension for up to three days. A cooling-off period. Only the Head can suspend, and must inform the parents in writing, the chair of governors and the LEA. Parents must return with the child at the end of the period to plan what to do in future.
8 Suspension leading to exclusion. Parents have the right to appeal. Full details of suspension and exclusion procedure are laid down in the LEA guidelines.

It must be stressed that constant drawing of attention to a child's misdemeanors and mistakes in a negative and punishing way may lead to an increase in his unacceptable behaviour. Opportunities for discussion and sharing ideas on working with children whose behaviour causes concern are available through the internal review system. Help and support are available from senior colleagues.

5 *Working with parents*

Parents are entitled to a range of opportunities to participate in and be consulted about the education of their children. The knowledge and experience on offer from parents is often under-used by professionals who do not recognise what a valuable and vitally important resource they can offer. Where relationships have developed positively between parents and professionals the efforts have been well rewarded in terms of progress for children. Parents will usually have a great deal of first-hand experience of the problems exhibited by the child in school. It is through an open and honest sharing of those experiences that a clear picture of the real problems will emerge. The idea of parents as partners is far from new, but it is an area where a great deal of work needs to be done, not least with this group of children. Working with the young person's parents will require a sensitive, honest and open approach to the problems displayed. Discussion should focus on what exactly is happening and not rely on judgemental statements or the causes of particular problems.

A whole-school approach to working with parents will avoid problems caused by individuals trying on their own, often with the best will in the world, to solve problems with the parents, which may lead to an increase in anxiety and concern rather than help. For example, many parents and professionals feel the need for stated causes for the child's difficult behaviours. Although sometimes, by identifying the causes, a clear path forward will emerge, this is not as likely as people hope. A great deal of time and energy can be expended in investigating a child's background and early years in an attempt to identify an event or a sequence of events that could have triggered a much later response. The identification of triggers will be of little help, since it is not possible to change them once they have occurred; feelings of guilt suffered already by parents struggling to come to terms with their child's behaviour may be increased. Attention needs to be paid to ways of preventing other problems and of managing the existing ones. Well thought-out opportunities for discussion and in-service work with parents is vital in this area in order to increase understanding for both parents and professionals.

Parents should be given every opportunity to speak openly about their concerns and experiences in order to enter into a helpful and honest dialogue with professionals. The professional should be able to listen and learn, and to contribute with clear observations and ideas, confident that he is working within the school's framework, which should also include formal opportunities for the teacher to refer parents to more senior colleagues or to other professionals, as appropriate.

Information should be available to parents on all aspects of the school's life, the curriculum as well as the rewards, praise and sanctions policy. The school's anxiety about a child's progress or general behaviour can be dealt with more swiftly and more effectively the sooner the parents are informed and involved. Legal information must also be shared, such as the formal assessment procedure under the 1981 Education Act, parents' rights of appeal, as well as the regulations under the 1988 Education Reform Act for exempting children from the National Curriculum. Face-to-face discussion is a way of dealing sensitively with such complex and important issues and gives the parents the opportunity for true sharing and joint planning to meet the needs of their child.

When parents have not seen the problem experienced by the school, discussion is just as, if not more, vital. To be told about a deterioration in a child's behaviour in an end-of-term report can be a shattering experience, particularly if there is no opportunity to meet school staff to discuss it until the new term begins, perhaps as long as five weeks away. Equally damaging is to paint a positive picture because the parents 'have enough to worry about'. Parents have a right to clear, direct and honest reporting of children's progress and difficulties, worded reassuringly and giving practical, positive suggestions for a way forward. A balance must be struck between formality and familiarity, and confusing or irrelevant jargon must be avoided. The skills needed to communicate clearly, concisely, yet sensitively, with parents could form the basis of at least one INSET day. Improved communication could result in real progress in the development of positive working relationships.

There is a thin line between being supportive and helpful to parents and invading their privacy. Even if the need to gain information is vital to successful working with the child, the relationship with his parents needs to be based upon mutual trust and entered into with patience.

When the parents are only too aware of their child's behaviour problems extra attempts should be made to report his positive behaviours and progress, to explain in specific terms what the child does and to give practical proposals for ways forward. Although it is more difficult to report positively on progress of an extremely disturbed child, it is arguably more important for his parents to be given something positive to build on; the same applies with other teachers and child-care workers who need help and support to maintain motivation and a positive approach to working with the child. Any such report must be founded on realistic expectations and not raise false hopes for the parents. Attention should always be paid to the 'self-fulfilling prophecy'; if expectations are too low, it is likely that the child will under-function. If everyone is expecting disturbed behaviour at all times it is more likely to occur, because the child will be given fewer opportunities to succeed.

The way that new parents are introduced to the school will affect the future relationship between the school and home. Sensitivity will be needed when working with parents of a child who has only recently been assessed for a statement of special educational needs because of behaviour problems or learning difficulties. The parents may be feeling guilty about how they think they may have failed their child, anxious about the provision that is being made for their child and concerned about his long-term future. Similar concerns will apply to any new parents who know that their child has had difficulty in a previous school. The school therefore needs to be particularly patient and welcoming to new parents.

The value of the parent/staff association cannot be underestimated as a means of support to new parents and those who are experiencing difficulty with their child. The opportunity to meet with other parents who may share similar experiences can be a very useful support. The parent/staff association can be a useful vehicle for arranging training courses and workshops for parents and teachers together, in relation to different aspects of helping children overcome their behaviour problems. The school policy can include an expectation that the staff and parents believe it is important to take advantage of training opportunities in a joint way.

The whole-school policy on working with parents needs to take account of the varying cultural and linguistic needs of some families, particularly in inner city and urban areas. It may be necessary to enlist the help of an interpreter when working with parents who do not speak English, or to involve members of the local community in teaching staff about cultural differences in standards of behaviour. Consideration will need to be given to the area the school is in, the age and abilities of the pupils and the practical possibilities of close working relationships, such as the size of the catchment area and whether the school is day or boarding.

Undoubtedly, the principle that it is the shared responsibility of staff to foster the development of close working links with parents is the starting point of a successful and meaningful policy. Identification of opportunities for forging these links is the next stage. One school which had a large proportion of pupils with additional behaviour problems tackled the problem through identifying the avenues for communication with parents that could be developed. The school decided to list the range of people who may communicate with parents; this included the following professionals:

Teachers	Doctors/Medical	Head teachers
Assistants	Officers	Houseparents
Children	Psychologists	Social workers
Nurses	Speech therapists	School social
Education welfare	Physiotherapists	workers
officers	Secretaries	

Clearly, such a large number of adults could cause, at best, confusion to parents and, at worst, extreme anxiety. The school therefore organised a statement of the sorts of communication that different people might have with parents and clarified how the school-based staff might work consistently with parents. Agreed working procedures with other non-school based professionals were also drawn up; this process had the additional advantage of clarifying the roles of each professional who was working from the school or who was attached to it. It was recognised that school–home links could be made by various people at different levels; these levels were split into formal and informal communications with parents. The school aimed to include parents at both levels so that they would have a real involvement in all aspects of the life of the school. The two diagrams on the opposite page show the range of opportunities available through which meaningful communication can be developed.

The school went on to describe the styles of communication available and to be encouraged in each area, which were unique to that school.

6 Guidelines on strategies for managing behaviour

It is important for a school to establish the procedures through which the staff work when there is a child with a serious or worrying behaviour

Diagram 1 – Informal communications

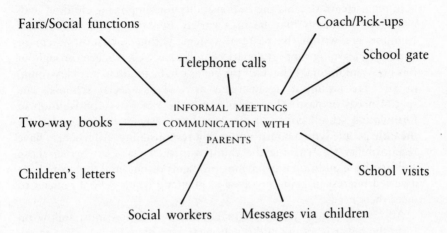

Diagram 2 – Formal communications

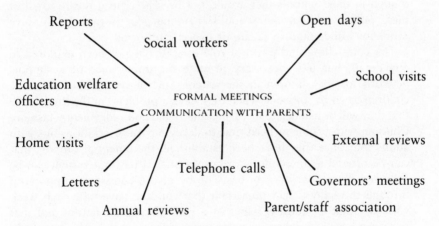

problem. People need to know what to do in terms of a management strategy, how to do it and who is responsible for sanctioning the programme. In order to address this issue, the school must respond to questions such as:

Are there guidelines on management strategies?
Is there a separate policy on restraint and withdrawal?
Who writes the guidelines/policies?
How often are they reviewed and updated?
Are they in line with LEA policy?

Are they in line with national thinking?
How does everyone know the school's policy?

In mainstream schools the responsibility for supporting children with behaviour problems may lie in a variety of settings. The three most common are within the pastoral system, within a faculty system or within the learning support department. But, as we have seen throughout this book, additional behaviour problems can be found in any classroom, in any age group, in mainstream as well as special schools. The special needs or pastoral teachers can make a positive contribution to formulating school policy in this area but must not be assumed to be the only people with a contribution or a responsibility. All teachers have responsibility for teaching the children in their classes, whether those children have additional behaviour problems or not, and therefore have a vested interest in being involved in planning whole-school policies to meet their needs.

Any whole-school policy on management strategies must follow on from the rewards, praise and sanctions statement and must relate to the aims and expectations of the school as a whole. It will also relate closely to policies on 'restraint and withdrawal', should these be necessary, though in most schools they would not be. The central theme to all of these policies is that the school's main purpose is to help to solve problems rather than to create or exacerbate them.

The counselling and pastoral role of staff has not been explored in any detail, but it is necessary to state the importance of a support network for the children in the school. Such a system should enable children to go to someone when they have a problem, in the knowledge that they will be listened to in a sympathetic and non-judgemental fashion. Children with problems need time to develop trusting relationships with adults, but once they have been established, the potential support that can be offered to the child is extensive. Such a pastoral system can be arranged on a year-by-year basis or by giving consistent support up through the school. It is important that children have time each week with an adult to address issues of a general pastoral nature and that they also have the right to request support from an individual adult. In such a system staff must expect to support children in their struggle to come to terms with themselves and to face the demands that society will place upon them when they reach adulthood.

One of the key reasons for a whole-school policy on management strategies is to avoid the stress suffered by staff who have to manage difficult children in isolation. Over-stressed adults are more likely to react physically with a child who is constantly challenging if they feel unsupported or believe it is necessary to prove that they can cope in any situation. The ability to recognise the need for help and the confidence to ask for help when it is needed will lead to a decrease in stress-related physical abuse of children. The senior staff in a school have a particular responsibility in this respect and need to make sure that support and development systems are sufficiently well planned and implemented to provide the back-up when needed. The support system for teachers should provide for a regular time each week for teachers to meet with senior colleagues. A mechanism needs to be built in to ensure that teachers are aware of their entitlement to ask for practical help and to make sure that entitlement is responded to.

The responsibility of senior staff extends further to the implementation of disciplinary proceedings against any member of staff who abuses children. The responsibility of all staff in this respect is to ensure the safety and quality of provision for children. The rules in relation to abuse must be clearly stated and, as with all rules, the consequence of breaking them must be fully understood by all concerned. A clear statement must be made available to all staff about unacceptable physical contact with children.

Abuse of children

Under no circumstances are children to be physically or sexually abused.

In order to protect children, the law clearly outlines illegal physical acts which are interpreted by LEAs into statements of authority policy on levels of acceptable punishment.

Corporal punishment is illegal. Any physical contact with a child can be interpreted as assault and it is therefore essential that staff establish the boundaries for necessary contact, such as the use of physical restraint and the circumstances in which it can be employed.

The guidelines on appropriate physical restraint are available in the staff handbook.

Stress on staff can be considerable when working with children which is why there is a support network established in the school. If you are unable to cope with a situation or feel that you are losing control, stand back and ask for help. Adults available for support and help are identified in the support and development manual.

Details of the sort of consideration to be paid in relation to physical restraint and isolation have been covered in detail in the previous chapter. Guidelines can be drawn up for a whole school policy based on the information described but as with every potentially difficult area of management, it is as well to check the statement with Governors and officers of the LEA. It is vitally important to clarify procedures on such issues for the safety and protection of children and staff alike; the dangers of potential misuse are considerable.

The following section is taken from one school's guidelines for management strategies; this school did in fact have guidelines on withdrawing children and in extreme circumstances on restraint procedures, but their suggestions have already been covered in detail. It was an all age special school which was organised into a primary and secondary department with class teachers for primary and form tutors for secondary classes, with secondary pupils moving round to different subject bases.

The role of the class teacher

The key person for welfare and discipline is the class teacher or form tutor. That teacher takes an over-view of all aspects of the child's education.

He is the link person to work with parents on day-to-day issues. Formal meetings with parents will be arranged through the Head or deputy.

He is responsible for calling an internal review on any child in his class who is causing concern, either because of his behaviour or as a result of particular learning difficulties.

He asks for this review through the deputy who is head of department. The class teacher is responsible for presenting written reports for the review meeting and for collecting information from other teachers as necessary.

Tutorial time is to be used daily to build relationships with the class, reinforce the school's rules and to deliver the core of the personal and social education programme.

Opportunities must be developed for pupils to contribute their views on the school, the curriculum and organisation. The class teacher is responsible for feeding back positive suggestions and ideas to staff meetings.

Behaviour problems in class should always be dealt with by the class teacher. The form teacher should be brought in at the next stage. If the problem is serious or persistent, it should be referred to the deputy head or the Head.

The referral system

Except in the case of serious or persistent behaviour problems, the role of senior staff is to advise, support and help colleagues in the day-to-day implementation of behaviour strategies. It is *not* their role to take children out of class for minor offences.

When a child is referred for an internal review, the deputy head will chair the meeting and will follow up with any recommendations after the meeting.

The deputy head will discuss new problems with the Head, and will give progress reports as necessary to the Head and the parents of any child with ongoing problems.

Recommendation for new involvement of support services will be sanctioned by the Head, with the full knowledge and support of the parents.

If staff are very concerned about a child's behaviour they will need to record incidents fully in writing to form the basis of professional discussions on how to manage and support the child.

The overall guidelines agreed by this staff had other sections on the personal and social education programme (arranged as a whole-school, cross-curricular delivery), record-keeping and reporting, as well as rewards, praise and sanctions. The policies were made available through the staff handbook, which was updated annually as part of the school review.

7 *Staff support and development system*

The class teacher can learn a wide variety of organisational and management skills for use within the classroom. He must have the support of other members of staff for professional growth, guidance and as a sounding-board for anxieties, frustrations and new ideas. There has been a danger of the teacher who copes well becoming as isolated as many parents, without clearly defined support systems. The advent of organised staff support and development systems and the introduction of structured appraisal should allow an early identification of need in the teacher as well as need in the child.

The Elton Committee welcomed the government's intention to introduce appraisal schemes for all teachers within a period of three to four years from September 1989, because the Committee believed that appraisal would lead to greater openness amongst teachers generally, and in issues relating to management of behaviour problems.

'We consider that the ability to relate to pupils and the standards of classroom management should be important elements of any appraisal scheme. Because of the critical part played by a teacher in classroom control, we would emphasise the need for appraisal to be supportive rather than threatening.'

The Elton Report, p 80, para 58

Interestingly, this view was not presented as one of the 173 recommendations made by the Committee, but the suggestion that formal appraisal schemes should pay close attention to classroom management skills of teachers was one area where the government responded immediately. It is important, therefore, that formal appraisal schemes should include an important element relating to management of children and classroom discipline. In order to avoid the potentially threatening aspect of appraisal it is crucial that in-school systems for staff support and development are seen as a priority.

An organised staff support and development system will give teachers practical and positive help within the classroom, will teach skills in self-appraisal and will incorporate ways of identifying professional strengths and needs, and then providing INSET to meet those professional needs. Such a system should aim to ensure sensitivity in working relationships based on positive and structured help rather than criticism and negativism.

Increasing knowledge and confidence in strategies for self-evaluation allow the teacher to assess when help or support is needed. The tendency to leave well alone when a situation seems calm can result in unnecessary stress and anxiety for the teacher or parent. Whole-school policies must therefore include careful monitoring of all staff. The ability to ask for help is dependent upon the individual's being confident that the request will not be greeted with criticism or ridicule.

The following list shows part of a school's self-evaluation checklist. The questions give a clear indication of the areas considered important by the writer, and provide a sound starting point for the class teacher's process of positive self-evaluation.

Class control and management

1 Do I arrive on time to lessons?
2 Do I prepare properly to teach each class?
3 Do I include a variety of activities for the whole ability range in the class?
4 Do I finish lessons on time and dismiss the children in an orderly fashion?
5 Do I speak to children with respect?
6 Is my behaviour a good model for children?
7 Do I make my expectations clear, eg, acceptable noise levels, standards of work, etc?
8 How often do I use praise for acceptable behaviour?
9 Am I fair in my expectations of individual children?
10 Do I anticipate possible causes of behaviour problems and try to prevent them?
11 Do I get involved in confrontation situations? If so, what do I do to avoid them happening again?

12 Do I know when I need help?
13 Am I prepared to ask for help or advice from colleagues when I need it?
14 Am I prepared to give help and advice to colleagues when they ask for it?
15 When using sanctions, do I
   i avoid arguing with the child
   ii make sure the child really is at fault
   iii explain the reasons for the punishment
   iv explain how the child can avoid the problem in the future?
16 Do I discuss discipline and management issues with colleagues and senior staff?

Teachers in special schools have traditionally had more experience of working with a group of children with another adult (or, in some cases, a number of adults) in the classroom. Teachers who have experience of team teaching will have overcome the initial embarrassment and anxiety suffered by those teachers who have only closed the classroom door to be alone with their children. Distant memories of

being a student, with the tutor observing a lesson, scribbling furiously and then telling you where you are going wrong;

or the probationary year, when the Head and Inspector spend short periods of time in the classroom and have no time to feed-back until the end-of-year report;

the full school inspection where everyone knows they are being watched at all times

are often the only experience that many teachers have of external observation of their work. These examples should not be termed 'appraisal' because they are not part of a structured and sensitive staff support and development system. Senior staff in schools and the Inspectorate will need to pay close attention to the way systems are introduced and presented in order to preserve staff morale and ensure that teachers learn and develop positively through the exercise.

A school system of frequent shared-teaching situations with peers and more senior colleagues, incorporating practical support as well as constructive feedback will help identify areas of need with teachers. Such an approach will ensure that opportunities are given to share ideas and strategies for more appropriate management. The need to observe behaviour and interactions between teachers and pupils, and pupils and pupils can be included in shared-teaching situations. The overall management and organisation of the school should take into account the need for teachers to work together in the classroom. It is easy for the visitor to the classroom to be critical; it is not as easy to establish a more appropriate style of management.

One of the most difficult areas to tackle when working with a group of children who display additional behaviour problems is the need to be aware of what each child is doing at each moment. The importance of staying one step ahead cannot be stressed too much. The teacher who is struggling in such a situation will often have missed many of the clues that the children give out before becoming disruptive. For example the child who asks for help and is not heard may well ask again, but is more likely to give up, pushing his book away, and then when the attention is finally given, refuse to try again. The inability to wait may be a contributing factor to the severity of a perceived behaviour problem. The additional adult observing in the classroom has a chance of identifying potential problems before they arise.

Parents and students are a valuable source of class support and, with careful planning, can take the role of observer. The Head teacher's role should incorporate joint teaching with colleagues as part of the support and development system – a far more valid use of time than teaching alone with a class of children. As with all aspects of this system, the Head teacher's involvement needs to be structured, with clearly stated and shared expectations.

Systematic observation of classroom practice will help to identify ways of meeting the needs of all the children in the class. As described above, potential problems can be identified by such monitoring, teachers can have positive and practical feedback on their delivery of the planned curriculum and, perhaps most importantly, appropriate advice and support can be given to manage behaviour problems in situ. This level of classroom observation would need to be undertaken by a senior member of staff or the Head in part of a formal appraisal system as it would be a formal part of staff development. However, colleagues should be encouraged to develop such strategies together for personal development. It will be effective only if the observer and the class teacher both know clearly what is being observed, and for this reason an agreed chart could form the framework. A copy of the completed chart should be given to the teacher and should include practical suggestions, advice offered and action to be taken.

The overall content of an observational schedule will vary from school to school, but the principles remain the same. When examining classroom practice in relation to management of behaviour problems in children with learning difficulties, the following considerations should be taken into account:

Preparation

1 Are the resources available?
2 Are they appropriate to the age of the children?
3 Are the learning objectives clearly stated?
4 Where does the activity fit into the work programme?
5 Is there evidence of the pupil's previous work at the appropriate developmental level.
6 Are the activities appropriate to the needs of the children?
7 Is the environment supportive to learning?
8 Are support staff appropriately deployed?

Delivery

1 How positive are the relationships between adults and children?
2 How involved are the children in the activity?
3 How are support staff used?
4 Is the style of teaching appropriate to the lesson being taught?
5 Is what was planned being taught?
6 Do the children have something to get on with when they have finished?

Evaluation

1 Were the learning objectives achieved?
2 Has each child's work been acknowledged?
3 Has progress been recorded?
4 How were behaviour problems managed?

The person doing the observation will be able to examine the provision in relation to similar questions and as a result will be able to make accurate statements rather than general judgements based on impressions. The next stage would be to discuss the observations with the teacher concerned and suggest practical ways to ensure that what is planned is appropriate and can be delivered.

CLASSROOM OBSERVATION SCHEDULE

TEACHER _____ CLASS _____ DATE _____
ACTIVITY _____ ABSENCES _____ TIME _____

1 ENVIRONMENT – Organisation and appearance

2 LESSON PREPARATION – Objectives and planning

3 LESSON/ACTIVITY – Sequence, content, teaching style

4 RESOURCES

5 PUPIL INVOLVEMENT

6 RELATIONSHIPS AND CLASS MANAGEMENT

7 MARKING AND RECORD KEEPING

8 PRACTICAL SUGGESTION, ADVICE AND ACTION TO BE TAKEN

---

8 *Reviews of individual children*

There are two key aspects of reviews; first, the legal requirements under the 1981 Education Act which referred to special needs; second, the on-going reviews needed by individual children. It is important to have a whole-school structure to ensure that the needs of individual children are kept under regular review. Reviews can be formal or informal and will involve a different group of children according to the needs of the child. If the child has a statement of special educational needs, under the 1981 Education (Special Needs) Act, there will be a legal requirement to have his statement reviewed at least annually.

To comply with the law, the school will need to work out a system to review the progress of each child against the educational provision that has been made. It will review the child's progress during the previous year and will set priorities for learning for the forthcoming year. These priorities or targets may include behavioural expectations and will specify resources that are necessary to achieve the priorities. The annual review will collate information and reports from all interested parties and every effort should be made to include parents in the review procedure. Schools will need to plan the timing of such meetings according to local considerations, such as the ability of parents to get to school, or the availability of professionals such as the speech therapist, educational psychologist and medical officer. The attendance of all the interested professionals will probably not be necessary for all children, but a report should be submitted to the meeting so that all advice is considered.

Under the 1981 Act, every child with a statement needs to have his needs re-assessed at $13\frac{1}{2}$ to ensure that the educational provision is meeting his stated needs. The $13\frac{1}{2}$ re-assessment results in the formation of a new statement, which is the result of advice from the parents, the school, the educational psychologist, the medical officer and the social worker. This review is done at $13\frac{1}{2}$ in order to plan for the last two years of statutory schooling, with a view to ensuring that the pupil has an appropriate education to prepare him for leaving school.

In addition to the reviews of a child's statement, there needs to be a system of on-going review for children with additional behaviour problems and learning difficulties. Staff need to know how to arrange a review when they are concerned about a child's behaviour and progress, and time should be set aside when these review meetings can take place. Such a meeting should involve all the staff who are working with that child, if an attempt is made to establish a consistent management policy, and a system for informing all other staff of the outcome of the review must be integral. All meetings should have an open agenda to which any member of staff can add an item to be minuted, with a section for action to be taken which also includes the person responsible for taking that action. Decisions made at any meeting must be shared with all members of the staff group. It is not always necessary to spend long periods of time on these reviews, but they do need to be held regularly and chaired strictly in order to stay on task.

The review system in a school acts as part of the staff support and development system, since the opportunity to get together with colleagues in a professional discussion can take some pressure off the class teacher. It gives the opportunity for staff to share ideas and make suggestions in a structured meeting and thus has an in-service training element. As with all aspects of behaviour management, it is important to deal with problems as early as possible in order to prevent them from escalating unnecessarily. The review procedure will do this by monitoring closely the needs of individual children. In some cases the number of reviews called by an individual teacher will indicate his need for additional support. Reports for reviews should always be written in a professional manner and in easily understandable language. Descriptions of behaviour problems, as we have seen, need to be accurate statements of what happens. Incident sheets should be attached, as necessary, to indicate antecedents, background to the behaviour and consequences so that there is a starting point for planning an intervention strategy.

The content of the report will depend on the reason for the review. Annual reviews and 13½ re-assessment reviews will demand detailed reporting of the stage the child has reached in all curriculum areas, as well as a section on emotional and social development and general behaviour. The internal, informal review is more likely to be concentrating on a specific area of the child's development and therefore will need reports or records that relate particularly to that area of concern. These might include examples of the child's work, the class teacher's profile record or copies of the child's positive behaviour record. Entries in two-way books between the teacher and parents can be a useful source of information for focusing on the child's behaviour. Whatever information is written about the child in school must be available to parents and written in a professional, clear and unambiguous way.

A central record needs to be kept of the frequency of reviews held on individual children. There is a danger that the only children discussed in a review setting are those with the most severe behaviour problems, who cause high levels of anxiety to staff. Children who do not have overt behaviour problems will also have particular needs in terms of their learning and general behaviour. For example, the child who does not attend in class but who is not particularly disruptive as a result, has as much right to have his needs reviewed as the disruptive, non-compliant person sitting next to him. It is easy to overlook children who seem on the surface to be getting on quietly with their work.

School policy on reviews

Formal reviews

Annual reviews, 13+ re-assessments, leavers' reviews and social services reviews will be held on Thursday mornings and will involve the child's parents, the class teacher and the Head teacher. (The social worker, speech therapist, physiotherapist, educational psychologist, school nurse and probation officer will be invited as necessary.)

Written reports are to be submitted to the deputy head for discussion two weeks before the meeting. Reports will be typed and circulated before the review. Examples of the pupil's work are to be brought to the meeting. The school secretary will minute the meeting.

Students are welcome to attend their leaver's review; younger children can attend part of their reviews, as appropriate.

Informal/Internal reviews

Reviews will be held on Tuesday and Friday mornings between

9.00 and 9.30 in the staffroom. These meetings can be called by any member of staff who is concerned by a child's behaviour or progress. The deputy head convenes these meetings. Forthcoming internal reviews are posted in the staffroom and recommendations are added at the end of the meeting.

An information sheet will be circulated to all staff in advance of the meeting to explain why the child is being reviewed.

Staff are asked to bring examples of incident sheets, behaviour programmes and profiles to the meeting. The class teacher should also bring a copy of the previous minutes relating to the child.

PLEASE BE PROMPT TO ALL MEETINGS – THERE IS LIMITED TIME AVAILABLE
THANK YOU

9 *Communication systems*

In order to meet the needs of children with behaviour problems and the staff who work with them it is necessary to have simple, clear systems of communication. There are two key types of communication system within the school; first, the whole-school systems such as curriculum, organisation, staff meetings, pastoral discussions and planning for INSET; second, those systems which relate to the needs of individual children, such as reviews, reports, incident sheets, etc. These systems meet the needs of all staff to know what is going on without being inundated with information that is of no interest to them. The balance between knowing enough to work positively as an active member of staff and having so much to read that nothing is taken in is a difficult one to keep.

Communication can be both informal and formal. Informal communication occurs throughout the school day; conversation in the corridor or staffroom, hand-over between parents and teachers, teachers and coach guides, child-care staff and teachers, etc. While the interactions may be valid, the nature of informal communications cannot be relied upon to form a substantial part of the school system of acceptable communication. Quite simply, there is no check or record of this type of interaction and therefore no opportunity to monitor the usefulness of it to the child. Often casual communication is unuseful, if a child posing the most severe problems is discussed at every opportunity, to the point where adults are looking for problems and possibly blaming him for something that he was not even involved in. Informal communication can lead to negative and unhelpful statements being made about a child.

Small schools (special and mainstream) have often functioned as a close-knit, friendly unit where daily information is passed on from one member of staff to the next. The knowledge that the Head, for example, will see everyone by morning break has been considered sufficient for the smooth running of the school. Such informal communication cannot be relied upon when trying to meet the needs of children with additional behaviour problems because of the danger that interactions between adults are in response to crisis rather than part of a planned programme of monitoring and intervention.

In a larger school or where the problems are more complex the volume of information that needs to be shared is far too great to work in an informal way. Heads of small schools are inundated with as much information from LEAs, the government and other parties as are their mainstream colleagues, and are now unable to continue the traditional practice of being the key disseminator of information. Development of a whole-school approach to communication will improve the development of all aspects of the school life and, most particularly, the ability of the school to support children with special needs and behaviour problems. The Elton Committee stressed the importance of effective communication systems:

> Poor communication is generally recognised as a feature of bad management. Our evidence suggests that communication with and between staff is particularly important for maintaining the kind of morale and atmosphere necessary to promote good behaviour.
> *Discipline in Schools*, 1989, p 93, para 22

The establishment of an effective system of communication to ensure that the needs of children with behaviour problems are met will depend upon the school's response to the following questions:

1 *What* information needs to be communicated?
2 *Who* needs to be informed or would like to be informed?
3 *How* should the information be communicated?
4 *When* should the information be communicated?

The school's formal communication systems should be designed in response to those questions and will therefore provide the structure and framework through which adults can communicate professionally and effectively. The same principles of designing an effective communication system will underly all aspects of communication in the school. For the purpose of illustrating one school's response to communicating effectively to meet the needs of children with learning difficulties and additional behaviour problems, the following school policy statement has been included.

Note There are examples in other chapters of forms referred to below.

Communication system

It is important to communicate in a clear, accurate and informed manner when discussing the needs of children. When an individual management programme is written for a child, the communication system needs to be included, taking note of what is to be communicated, to whom, when, and the means of that communication. The following guidelines are intended to form the basis of our formal communication systems.

What should be communicated?

1 All behaviour reports should be open to parents.
2 Details of family circumstances must not be included in school reports.
3 Incidents should be reported factually, using the forms available (Chapter 3, pp 79–80)
4 Accidents/injuries to children must be reported in the accident book and an incident sheet completed. (Chapter 3, pp 79–80)
5 Accidents/injuries to staff must be reported in the accident book and an incident sheet completed.
6 Behaviour management programmes must be clearly stated, with the targets communicated to all (Chapter 3, pp 81–85)
7 The outcome of the programme needs to be communicated, emphasising progress, and including modifications to the programme.
8 Completed behavioural observation schedules need to be made available.

Who needs to be informed?

This will depend upon the information being communicated, however, the following people need to be considered:
1 The parents have a right to know what is happening with their child and need to be kept fully informed.
2 The Head needs to be informed in writing of any serious or unusual incident.
3 Other teachers and non-teaching staff need to receive copies of new programmes, serious incident forms and management strategies.
4 Other professionals (education welfare officer, social worker, educational psychologist, therapist, medical officer, etc) will need reports from time to time and may need to be informed of particular aspects of the child's school life. If in doubt, check with the deputy head first.
5 The Head teacher will inform governors of general behaviour

management issues through the Head's report to governors. Extreme situations requiring suspension or exclusion must be cleared by the Head through the chair of governors.

How should information be communicated?

In most situations, communication needs to be in writing. When information is passed on verbally, either in face-to-face discussion or on the telephone, a written record must be made afterwards in the child's file. The following form the main types of written communication:

1 Letters home, written by the Head, the class teacher (cleared by the head of department), the therapist, etc.
2 Letters to professional colleagues, written by the Head, often covering a school report.
3 School reports.
4 Bulletins on the notice board (Individual Children section).
5 Incident summarised on the board in the staff room (factual information).
6 Through agendas and minutes of staff meetings, or internal and external reviews. All meetings must have agendas and be minuted. Minutes must be displayed on the minutes board in the staffroom.
7 Through two-way books between home and school – an on-going diary between the class teacher and the parents.
8 Through the home-work book.

When should information be communicated?

As an underlying principle, information needs to be communicated as soon as possible. In the case of a serious incident, for example, parents will need to be informed immediately with a follow-up letter. This would be done by the Head or senior member of staff on duty. Care should be taken not to cause unnecessary concern to parents by informing them of trivial incidents. If in doubt, check with the head of department or Head.

1 Some information will need to be communicated regularly, eg, weekly report on the child's behaviour.
2 Review reports will be required • as requested by the parents for re-assessment • for annual reviews • for 13+ statutory re-assessments • for school-initiated re-assessment.
3 Annual reports will be written on all children in each subject area.

10 In-service training – INSET

Teachers undoubtedly spend a disproportionate amount of time working with the children who are most demanding; if that time could be channelled into more effective teaching and management there would be less frustration experienced by teachers and more progress made by children. The support available to staff through a structured in-service training programme (provided through school-focused INSET and training opportunities provided by external agencies) is crucial to the success of meeting the behavioural needs of children.

For the first time the whole question of INSET for teachers has become a national priority through the local education authority training grants scheme (LEATGS). Expenditure of the grant has been decided by LEAs under broad headings laid down by the secretaries of state for education and has covered issues such as the National Curriculum, management training for Heads and senior staff and 'shortage' subject areas such as science and technology. The Elton Committee made a very strong recommendation to the government that one of the most important areas for priority LEATGS funding was that of in-service training in classroom management and organisation. The committee believed this to be one of the most crucial influences on the development of effective classroom practice. They felt so strongly about the importance of this initiative that the Committee recommended that priority funding should last for five years until at least 1994/95. The government responded by making the management of pupil behaviour a national priority in 1990/91.

Each school will need to make its own priorities in regard to in-service training for teachers and non-teaching staff. The overall direction and organisation of the school-based INSET programme is the responsibility of the Head teacher working closely with the staff group. The INSET programme will be planned for the identified individual, group and whole-school needs and will change from year to year as school experience and knowledge develops. The on-going review of any school should include attention to the in-service training needs of staff in relation to managing children's behaviour. The seriousness of behaviour problems displayed in any particular school will affect the level of priority given to behaviour management training.

Even with the recommendation by the Elton Committee that initial training for teachers should include detailed attention to practical issues relating to classroom management and school discipline, it is unreasonable to expect the initial training course to equip teachers for a whole career in education. Schools can help student teachers during their teaching practice and licensed teachers during their training to gain insight into issues relating to management of children with behaviour problems; indeed, the availability of whole-school policies for students will not only provide a clear expectation for them while they are in the school, but will also provide examples that can be taken back into college for discussion. The period of induction during the first year of a new teacher's career provides a unique opportunity for senior teachers to share their skills and knowledge of the practical setting with the first-year teacher while monitoring his progress. Such on-going support is a valuable source of school-focused in-service training and will, if used sensitively and within a structured framework, form a basis for future monitoring and self-appraisal. It is during the initial years of teaching that the development of classroom management skills really takes place.

Similar in-service training opportunities should be provided in school in order to concentrate on practical ways for teachers to motivate and manage groups as well as individual children. One of the most valuable opportunities to 'develop patterns of mutual support amongst colleagues' has been through the introduction of 'Baker days'. The five in-service training days to be used for school-based training each year has given much needed time for focusing on priority areas in the school, either as a whole staff or in groups decided by the Head and staff. Time has been available to review the school's position in relation to management of children with behaviour problems, rewards, praise and sanctions as well as teaching and classroom methodology. Many schools have used their in-service budget to pay for visiting speakers and some have arranged to join together with neighbouring schools for cross-phase discussions and planning. The developing understanding and awareness of the problems faced by colleagues in different schools and in different classes in the same schools has been invaluable in developing patterns of mutual support. Future plans for school-focused in-service training will need to include aspects of classroom management and management of behaviour problems.

The Head teacher's role in relation to school-focused in-service training is to match the perceived needs of staff with the identified needs of the children and the school. In order to achieve this efficiently, the school rather than outside agencies needs to be seen as the 'provider' of in-service opportunities for the staff. One of the underlying principles of this book has been the emphasis upon teachers and parents having, or being able to learn, the skills necessary to meet the needs of the children. A close examination of the skills and strengths of existing staff members will pay dividends when looking for individuals to lead in-service training sessions. Not only can the member of staff share his skills with colleagues, but the process of preparing himself to lead such a workshop will be a valid and useful INSET opportunity for self-appraisal, particularly if the Head or senior member of staff takes the time to talk through the contribution the teacher is expected to make.

A school staff confident in leading workshops with colleagues can begin to develop the resource centre concept, where a school (sometimes in a special school) provides in-service opportunities to local schools and teachers in particular areas of expertise. Management of behaviour problems and class teaching methodology will be one area where special school staff especially can make a positive contribution.

The retrospective report below covers one school's INSET arrangements aimed at broadening experience and knowledge in relation to behaviour management issues. The programme lasted one year, initially, and provided a firm starting point for the on-going review of behaviour management in the school.

Behaviour management INSET

The focus on behaviour management was identified as a whole-school priority because of expressed concerns by all staff over levels of disruption, high stress amongst staff and the belief that children were not achieving as well as could be expected. All teachers agreed to focus on this aspect of the school's development and to contribute to the INSET programme.

1 Introductory meeting

During the first meeting in September, the Head lead the discussion to formulate the aims of the INSET and agree the programme for the year. The Head also talked about classroom management strategies. He gave each teacher a paper relating to classroom management, for reference.

2 Weekly teachers' meetings

Each week, one child was focused upon in an effort to make positive plans to manage his behaviour. There was usually an obvious child to discuss, but efforts were made to include children who did not cause the most overt problems.

3 Case study

Each month a different teacher presented a case study during the curriculum meeting. There were ten teachers plus the Head, so everyone had a turn. The case study had to be on a child taught by that teacher, and had to include:

- an accurate and factual description of the child's problems,
- a list of the child's strengths and interests,
- a statement of what had been tried already,

- at least two detailed incident sheets, showing antecedents, behaviour/background and consequences.

The whole staff then analysed the information provided and jointly agreed a management programme. The first ten minutes of the next case study meeting was used to evaluate the effectiveness of the programme.

4 Baker day

One Baker day was put aside for the school educational psychologist to talk about the use of praise and rewards as a positive approach to behaviour management. With his involvement, the staff agreed a whole-school approach to praise, rewards and sanctions.

5 Courses

Each teacher attended a course or made a visit as part of his own professional development. This had to relate to an issue to do with behaviour management and the teacher concerned was expected to provide each colleague with a hand-out on what had been learnt and/or observed. He then fed back to a staff meeting to enable discussion to take place about his visit. Subjects covered included:

- a token economy in an EBD [emotional and behavioural difficulty] school
- pastoral care in a mainstream secondary school
- working with parents
- breaking down teaching tasks into manageable steps
- record-keeping and reporting
- team and paired teaching
- classroom management techniques
- time out
- the management of stress
- positive and negative reinforcement
- Continual assessment procedures
- Teacher self-appraisal

The Head teacher helped to arrange visits and made sure that all staff were aware of courses outside the school. All teachers wrote and circulated a report of their visit or course to their colleagues. A central record of these reports was kept for future reference.

6 Evaluation and review

The last teachers' meeting of the school year was used to evaluate the effectiveness of the programme. The following statements were made:

1 All teachers said they knew more about the practical ways of managing children with behaviour problems.
2 There was a positive policy in place on a whole-school approach to rewards, praise and sanctions.
3 Teachers felt they were working far more as a team and had gained in understanding of each other's problems.
4 The response to individual children was more consistent and appropriate in terms of realistic expectations.
5 There were more positive links being made with parents – this was measured by the number of parents working in the classroom now, the numbers attending meetings on children and the decrease in letters of complaint.
6 Most importantly, the overall behaviour of the children had improved – there was a decrease in reported incidents even though the recording system was tighter – and staff generally felt under less stress.

The final part of the meeting was spent in discussing where the staff group could go next to consolidate what had been learnt and to continue to improve management strategies with children.

This example goes much of the way to both building up the skills of the staff and addressing a whole-school approach. With the demands for training in so many areas, however, it will be difficult for any school to repeat such a course within a given time scale. Each school needs to establish a basic training package for all its staff to ensure that they gain basic skills to handle behaviour problems. The essential areas that should be covered by all staff are:

– child development and behaviour problems
– classroom organisation and management
– establishment of behaviour modification programmes
– establishment of praise, rewards and sanctions systems
– classroom observation procedures
– the physical handling of pupils
– record-keeping procedures
– managing other staff in the classroom
– team-teaching strategies

It is also appropriate to suggest that when such INSET is being planned it will be most effective to offer a flexible range of learning strategies, and to match the needs of individual teachers to the particular strategies. A flexible strategy will enable a higher level of course member organisation and participation. Any programme should incorporate at least four main activities:

1 *Core lectures*	— These may include discussions and work exercises, and can incorporate outside speakers.
2 *Individual study*	— A study or a negotiated topic by each individual on the course programme.
3 *Group study*	— Each individual should be allocated to work with a small group of colleagues. As well as joining other sessions, the group would focus their attention on a particular aspect of development.
4 *Seminars*	— These should provide the individual with the opportunity for personal attention and discussion.

Having examined a range of whole-school policies which are essential when aiming to meet the needs of children with learning difficulties and behaviour problems, it is necessary to look at organisational influences on positive management.

5
How can we manage it?

Introduction

Having established that a range of policies incorporating a consistent response from all staff and parents is necessary, the question of internal organisation needs to be tackled. There are various aspects of organisation that can affect the school's ability to meet the needs of an individual or group of children. Attention needs to be paid to:

- organisation and allocation of staff
- the use of the building and accommodation
- movement around the building
- access to particular areas and facilities
- breaks and lunchtimes
- health and safety

1 Working with other adults

There is a wide range of issues that needs to be considered in relation to working with other adults in order to meet the needs of children with additional behaviour problems, since it is the adults who will make or break a behaviour programme, and as we have seen in previous chapters, parents, teachers and non-teaching staff have different experiences of managing children as well as different tolerance levels of particular problems.

In most special-school classrooms there are more than one adult, often with strongly held, individual views on how to manage the children. Increasingly, classroom assistant support is given to children with statemented special needs in mainstream schools and working with more than one adult in the room is becoming more widespread. It is vitally important for the teacher to take a clear lead on the behaviour of the other adults in the room. Tension and irritation can grow between staff if areas of responsibility are not clearly agreed and laid down. It is possible to negotiate responsibility areas with a classroom assistant so that both adults clearly understand where their individual roles start and stop. In some instances the roles will overlap and that will need to be clearly stated to avoid confusion.

Adequate consultation time needs to be made available for the adults to plan programmes, and such liaison will be assisted by clearly written pupil assessments and work programmes. It will be helpful not only to be clear on the role of an additional adult within a classroom during a specific behaviour programme, but also to have a clearly agreed set of guidelines for such work.

1 Any individual support should be directly related to the lesson concerned; it is a matter of behavioural support to provide access to the curriculum.
2 A pupil should not normally be isolated from his peers.
3 The work of the support adult should not be distanced or different from the work of the teacher.
4 Other pupils in a class benefit from access to two adults.
5 A second adult enables an evaluation to be made of a pupil's response to another adult within the formal classroom situation.
6 Collaboration between the two adults should lead to a wider range of strategies being available for behavioural support within the classroom.

Who is responsible for what in the classroom needs to be communicated to the children also, since children sometimes try to play off one adult against another if they think they can get away with doing so. Clarity of lines of communication and areas of responsibility will allow one adult to respond to the child by saying 'You know Mr . . . is in charge of that. Go and ask him.' Children will soon learn who to ask for what, if the responses are consistent.

In some classrooms it will be necessary for the teacher and assistant to exchange roles at different times during the day, for example, when teaching or assessing toileting behaviour. The teacher may sometimes need to take all the children to the toilet in order to identify which targets should be worked on next. Or the assistant may be telling the whole class a story while the teacher concentrates on one child's individual language programme. Careful planning and clarification of expectations will enable this sort of organisation to work effectively.

It is even more crucial to decide in advance the roles of the adults when working with very disturbed children; should there be a serious incident, everyone needs to know what exactly they should do immediately. This is particularly important when someone needs to ask for help whilst ensuring the safety of the other children. In this situation it may be necessary to send a child for help from a named adult, or a parent or volunteer. This responsibility would need to be clarified in advance. The same sort of organisation is needed for the smooth management of less serious situations. If, for example, one adult is dealing with a situation and another takes over or joins in without being asked, the second person can cause more of a problem than provide any real help. As a general rule, the member of staff dealing with the problem should feel able to ask for help if it is needed and feel confident that his colleague will be on hand if necessary. The exception to this will be when a senior member of staff judges the teacher or child to be at risk and has no alternative but to take over.

The senior member of staff in this instance must be sensitive to the feelings of both the adult and the child, making sure that neither thinks the child has won. It will be important for the senior member of staff to return to the adult after the incident is over in order to talk through what has occurred and why it was necessary for him to take over. The other side of this coin is when an adult needs and wants help and another adult stands back, for fear of causing offence to the teacher. A simple system of asking for help and responding accordingly can help staff overcome such dilemmas. It may be necessary to stand by, offering support should the situation deteriorate. Often the appearance of a more senior, or different, member of staff can lead to a situation calming down and highlight a way of restoring order.

Other adults can be used to remove a child from a disrupted situation to allow a period of calm to resume in the classroom. This is useful when there is a group of children behaving in a disruptive manner and refusing to comply with the teacher. This situation can deteriorate if the teacher cannot regain control quickly. The temporary removal of, for example, the noisiest or the most disruptive child enables the teacher to be seen by the other children to be the one to restore order. This is important in terms of relationships; if the senior member of staff went into the classroom and calmed the children down, without changing the background or consequences, there is every chance that the behaviour would deteriorate again when he left. By removing one or two children, the teacher can regain control and will be in a position to receive the children back into a calm and working group.

On other occasions, it may be necessary to take a child away from the main class group for a number of individual teaching sessions, with the built-in expectation that he will return to the class afterwards. This style of organisation can be implemented either to reward the child for appropriate behaviour or to remove him whilst he is still behaving well, in the knowledge that he will not last much longer. If, for example, detailed observation and recording shows that the child behaves in an unsettled manner at around eleven every morning, the decision to take him elsewhere at a quarter to eleven is likely to remove the pressure from him and from everyone else in the class. It will also allow him to engage in an adult-led activity at which he can succeed. This sort of flexible use of staffing can be very successful in positively managing children with additional behaviour problems. As in the previous example, the child must be re-integrated into the main class group as an integral and important part of the programme.

As in all cases when a child is away from the classroom, it is important that the child accounts directly to the class teacher on return; this 'touching base' re-establishes the teacher as the person with prime responsibility to re-integrate the child into the group. It reinforces the teacher's authority and responsibility for the class as a whole.

More adults do not necessarily produce more effective management strategies. It is the effective deployment of adults that will help children overcome their behaviour problems, rather than the number of adults available in the classroom. Pressure on children can be increased by an increased staffing ratio; for some children this might be brought about by constant demands for acceptable behaviour that they cannot manage continually. This can result in an increase in the frequency and severity of the behaviour problem.

If the roles of adults in a classroom are not clearly agreed and stated there is a danger of adults sorting out what they are supposed to be doing in front of the children. The removal of attention and supervision from the task in hand can be enough to result in disruptive and unsettled behaviour. Take, for example, the only too common situation where a child is unable to get on with the activity that has been set and asks for help, only to be told, 'Wait a minute. Can't you see I'm talking?' He will probably wait for a minute, given a particular level of tolerance, but will then ask again and again be told to wait. It is most unlikely that he will wait for very long before he begins to disrupt the other children. He will then, of course, be told off and told to get on with his work, quietly. He is back to the problem he started with, except this time he has been told off as well.

The clarification of roles within the classroom is more complicated and potentially more difficult to manage when it involves a range of different professionals. Each professional is likely to make different demands on the child unless there is sensitive yet firm management on the part of the class teacher. It is necessary to establish working procedures from the outset to avoid professional conflict amongst the adults and confusion for the children. Many therapists coming into the classroom are only too aware of the difficulties of their role and are conscious of the disruption their presence may cause and would appreciate the opportunity to clarify working relationships. It would be unfortunate if there was a return to the therapist removing the child from the classroom for treatment and then returning him at the end of the session, with little opportunity for sharing knowledge or feeding back. It has been stressed throughout the book that children need additional support within the class setting rather than 'treatment' in another setting. Close working relationships and a shared understanding of the holistic goals for the child need to be established between professionals in order to achieve this.

It is sometimes easier to establish consistency when working with parents and volunteers in the classroom. Again, it is essential to share expectations and targets for the children with the other adult and to spend some time in explaining exactly what the teacher wants the parent/ volunteer to be involved in and how he is to work with the child. The more information is easily shared at the beginning of the session, the more smoothly the parents will fit in to the classroom. The importance of involving parents in the classroom cannot be stressed too much. Parents could be used in the following roles:

1 As a support in general classroom activities
2 As an observer
3 To work with individual children on special programmes
4 To work or play with a group whilst the teacher is freed to concentrate on an individual or small group
5 To demonstrate a successful way of working with their own child
6 To teach in the child's mother tongue

All these examples of ways in which parents can contribute to the work in the classroom will help the teacher to manage children with additional behaviour problems positively, given that the teacher is well organised and prepared and is clear about what he expects the parents to do. There are numerous examples of successful involvement of parents in classroom practice which reinforce the view that a little time given to sharing goals and expectations with parents will be time well spent.

Special needs support teachers are available in most schools to help children with learning difficulties or behaviour problems. The way that a support teacher approaches his work in the mainstream or special school setting will affect his ability to offer useful and worthwhile assistance. As we have seen with other professionals, the removal of the child from the class setting is unlikely to have a lasting effect on the child's behaviour when he returns to being one of a whole class. The support teacher will need to adapt his support to the classroom. This may not necessarily be to the child directly but to the teacher and so, indirectly, to the child. Support can be offered in areas such as helping the teacher to improve his self-esteem, to recognise success when it occurs and to grow in confidence in his ability to manage a class or a child.

The support teacher may work alongside the child with problems to help him gain access to the subject being taught. In an obvious example, the child who becomes disruptive because he cannot read is likely to be able to behave more appropriately if someone is able to give him the extra time and help to tackle the reading task. The support teacher may also observe what is happening and help the class teacher to write an appropriate management programme and then support him in implementing that programme. The support teacher can be used as a classroom assistant if the class teacher has sufficient confidence to lead the lesson clearly and direct another adult. In this situation the class teacher maintains the overall control of the class and the children look to him for instructions. The support teacher can be directed to potential problem areas and to children who are showing signs of difficulty. He should take at least a small group of children which includes the child with particular problems, rather than 'single out' the individual child. There is sometimes value in the support teacher taking the whole class and giving the regular class teacher the opportunity to observe his children working with another adult. In terms of behaviour management this can be an invaluable learning experience for the class teacher, not to mention an opportunity for that teacher to put his own classroom delivery into perspective.

All teachers have experienced the difficulty of just managing to settle a class of children to work when there is a knock at the door and the school nurse asks for children to come for medicals. The number of interruptions in a classroom during a week can be great and clearly very disruptive to children with already short attention spans and disturbed behaviour patterns. Every effort should be made to ensure that staff know about visitors so that they can plan around them. It is important to ensure that any visit to the classroom is essential; anything that can wait until break or after school should do so. When there is another adult available in the classroom, that adult can be given the responsibility of dealing with visitors rather than having to disrupt the class teacher. That adult can also be responsible for managing crises, incidents and emergencies so that the class can continue to work undisturbed.

In many boarding schools the key worker system provides the child with someone to relate with. The key worker is responsible for monitoring the child's progress as well as ensuring that management programmes are kept under review and are implemented according to plan. It is the key worker who acts as the link person with parents, particularly when they are unable to visit their child frequently. He makes sure that information is sent home and that the child writes regularly, if he is able to do so; the key worker writes on his behalf, if the child cannot write. The opportunity for the child in day school to have a 'named person' who knows all about him and who can be trusted can be seen as an extension of the key worker system. The importance of a key or pastoral worker throughout each phase of a child's school life is clear. As the child grows older the importance of being able to relate to and trust a particular adult increases the value of a pastoral system that runs throughout every year of secondary schooling.

The Head teacher needs to be aware of the extra pressures on staff which result from working with children with additional and severe behaviour problems. It is important to rotate staff over a period of time so that individuals have the chance to 're-charge their batteries' and to have a break from the continual demands of working with such children. In the same way that teachers may be tempted to leave a disturbed child alone when he is working quietly, so a Head may be tempted to leave the successful teacher of difficult children to carry on as long as he is working well. As with the child, it is when the teacher is working well and being successful that he needs to be rewarded. Too often teachers become disillusioned when working in very stressful situations because they feel their efforts are not appreciated; a sensitive Head will positively reinforce staff as he would positively reinforce children for effort and achievement.

Because such children are so demanding, the rewards for staff need to be built in, beyond the intrinsically rewarding nature of the work. Opportunities for short and long term courses should be made available as well as chances to change areas of interest to maintain motivation. It is a false economy to expect teachers who are successful at working with children who have additional behaviour problems to want to continue indefinitely. It is vitally important to train other colleagues in the skills necessary to work positively with such children, to make sure that the necessary support networks do not collapse if one teacher should leave. This task may be an area of professional interest and challenge to the successful teacher and could be extended beyond the school, into a wider LEA training brief.

Working with other adults can be fraught with difficulty, but clear lines of communication, shared goals and mutual support and understanding will lead to a team approach to meeting the needs of the children. This supportive approach, as we have seen, is likely to be the only successful way forward if the intention is to support children with behaviour problems alongside their peers.

KEY POINTS

- Communication and agreed working procedures are essential for positive classroom practice.

- All staff in the classroom need to know what they are responsible for and who they are responsible to.

- Children who are withdrawn from the classroom because of disruptive behaviour should be re-integrated as soon as possible.

- Extra adults in the classroom do not in themselves lead to more settled behaviour in the children.

- Support adults can make a positive contribution to the management of children with behaviour problems when used positively.

- Adults as well as children need positive reinforcement for effort and achievement.

2 *Maximum use of the building*

Many schools have antiquated buildings, are sited on main roads, have limited play space, have too few or badly positioned facilities and some raise the question, 'Purpose built – for what?' The fact remains that schools have to be worked and lived in, as do homes, in order to meet the needs of the children who are based there. To stand back and work out positively the strengths of the building, and then to identify what the staff need in order to do the job, helps to clarify exactly what improvements are essential. It also leads to a clear focus on the advantages of a particular building for the job in hand. A clearly formed and planned case for improvements to a building is likely to receive a more favourable response than a series of statements describing reasons why it is impossible to do the job.

The physical layout of the building cannot be altered overnight, but the imaginative use of aspects of the building can minimise potential problems with young people who display disturbed behaviour patterns and minimise the staff's management problems. For example, placing a junior class in a room next to the playground will minimise the chances of children absconding or being disruptive to others on the way to breaks. Siting class bases near the toilet areas will make it easier for children who have toileting problems.

Many schools do not have individual teaching areas that can be used to withdraw children, although from time to time they may be needed. As a general rule, however, children with behaviour problems should be taught within the classroom and not withdrawn to an artificial teaching situation. The re-settlement of the child into the main class group can cause as many problems of adjustment for the child, for the teacher and for the other children as the child caused before withdrawal.

Emphasis should be upon the planned use of resources rather than on crisis intervention when teaching has broken down. The examination of all physical resources is essential for use in a structured programme even when it seems at first glance that there are no spare rooms available. The way that areas of the school are timetabled may give opportunities for shared use of facilities and for children to work in smaller groups.

All children need the security of having their own base classroom, even if they are old enough to move to other areas of the school for certain lessons. The familiarity of a settled and organised base helps children to establish a routine within which the rules are clearly stated. They take an interest and pride in the class base environment and each child takes responsibility for some aspect of it. The way adults value and look after the environment will affect the levels of attention that children pay to the classroom, as well as to other areas of the school. The base classroom gives children a place where they feel they belong and, more importantly, where they can find their class teacher or form tutor. This room is an important part of the school's pastoral provision, so that children know where as well as to whom they can go if they have a problem.

There is no doubt that children will be less disruptive in a tidy, well organised school than they will be in one which is filled with clutter and rubbish. Careful organisation of centrally used resources and storage will not only make the school look cared for, but will keep valuable and/or dangerous equipment away from children who may play with it inappropriately. Stock cupboards should be kept locked if they house equipment that children can damage, destroy or hurt themselves with. For example, proper storage of PE equipment will prevent children from climbing and jumping without supervision; electrical equipment could be mis-used or broken if left around; and scissors, craft knives and staple guns should never be left out where children are not closely supervised. A review of the amount and siting of storage space will be useful when aiming to avoid unnecessary behaviour problems.

It may be helpful to undertake a complete review of all accommodation and resources as a whole-staff venture, both to share the information and to enable staff to offer suggestions for more creative use of space. The model below is taken from a draft schedule by Birmingham LEA to establish such an information base.

Accommodation, environment and resources

Teaching spaces

1 What is the planned use of all teaching space within the school?
2 What teaching spaces (if any) do not meet the needs of the learners?
3 To what extent are spaces adequately provided with necessary services?

Learning environment

1 What arrangements does the school have for making its site and buildings stimulating and interesting?
2 What arrangements are there to utilise the grounds, outdoor facilities and local environment as curriculum resources?

School site and grounds

1 To what extent are the buildings and site safe and clean?
2 What arrangements are there to assist visitors to the site?
3 To what extent is the site suitable for pupils/staff/visitors with disabilities?

Administration facilities

1 To what extent are the accommodation and facilities appropriate to the needs of the secretarial, clerical, technical, canteen and care-taking staff?
2 What administrative support is available for senior staff and postholders?
3 How is confidential information stored and accessed?
4 What medical facilities are available?
5 What is the office provision for pastoral staff/year heads?

Health and safety

1 What procedures exist for carrying out health and safety checks throughout the school?
2 What procedures exist for fire practices?

Allocation and control of resources

1 To what extent is the age and quality of resources appropriate to learners' needs in respect of
   – visual aids
   – reprographics
   – microtechnology?
2 What systems and criteria exist for the allocation of resources within the school?
3 What systems exist for resource storage, retrieval and distri-bution?
4 What methods of resource stock control and audit are used?

KEY POINTS

- Identification of the advantages of a building is more useful than concentrating on its weaknesses.

- Use of areas of the building should be reviewed regularly to ensure it is being used to its best possible advantage.

- Areas for individual and small-group teaching need to be identified.

- All children need a base room where they can keep their possessions and feel secure.

- Storage areas and stock cupboards need to be well used and kept in an orderly fashion to avoid mis-use of equipment.

3 Pupils moving around the building

Many difficulties seem to occur when children are transferring from one lesson to another, from one member of staff to another, or between parents and staff. At such times, the lines of responsibility for the child that are clearly laid down in normal circumstances are not in force and, therefore, the messages received by the child can be confusing. Attention needs to be paid to the supervision of children at such times to prevent problems from occurring.

Before school starts and at the end of the school day supervision is likely to be less strict and the support that the child receives throughout lesson times is missing. It is at these times that the support needs to be provided consistently and positively by a named person on duty to supervise children coming into the building in the morning and going out at night. If the children travel on school transport it is helpful to supervise them to and from the bus; children with severe behaviour problems will be closely supervised, of course, but those who 'get into trouble' during free times can often be kept in line by the knowledge that somebody is there and watching.

The movement of children who have aggressive outbursts through the building can lead to potentially dangerous encounters with other, perhaps younger or more vulnerable, children. The careful selection of the most appropriate class base, close to facilities needed by that group or individual, can minimise danger and significantly reduce the stress and anxiety of staff. The movement from one lesson to another needs to take into account not only the right of each class or individual to have access to the facility but also the physical paths taken by each group when moving from one lesson to another. Movement around the school is fraught with potential problems for the child who has difficulty in organising himself.

Careful attention to preparation for lessons will decrease the number of times that children have to leave the classroom during lesson time. One child going on an errand is unlikely to cause problems, but two or three children meeting in the corridor on the way to collect stock or equipment are much more likely to become disruptive. Children going to the toilet during class-based times are increasingly at risk of being involved in unacceptable activities. Children who require regular toileting will be supervised on the way to and in the toilet area, but other children need to be taught to wait until a time that is convenient to the teacher or until the end of the lesson. The fewer the opportunities for children to move freely around the building, the fewer the chances of children misbehaving or being distracted.

KEY POINTS

- Problems can be avoided if close attention is paid to the movement of children around the school.

- Children with extreme behaviour problems will need close supervision to ensure safety.

- Being prepared will avoid the need for children to leave the room during lessons to collect equipment.

4 *The right of access to facilities*

Access for children to all facilities will always need close attention to ensure that all children, no matter what their disability, have equal opportunity to be involved in all activities. The same attention needs to be paid to the timetable and routines when planning for children who have physical disabilities, either those who use wheelchairs or those with mobility problems. The ambulant, hyperactive or disorientated youngster can not only injure children who are physically less able, but can also instil feelings of fear and anxiety, perhaps resulting in withdrawal.

Many special schools find that it is easier to provide a segregated provision within the school for the most extreme children, maybe those who exhibit the most extreme behaviour problems, those children who have the most extreme physical needs or those who struggle with basic reading, writing and mathematics skills and cannot keep up with the rest of the class group. In each case the most extreme is relative to the population of the school: the most disturbed in one school might be considered amongst the most settled in another school. The grouping of children will say a great deal about the underlying philosophy of the school and can in some instances lead to self-fulfilling prophecy: that is, these children need additional support, are placed in a separate classroom to receive that support, and as a result are perceived by staff and children alike as different. They therefore behave differently and the gap between them and their peers widens. The criteria for grouping and class organisation need constant review by the staff group. The school which aims to integrate all children into the general class groupings will make every effort to ensure access for all, probably by sensitive and flexible use of human resources.

Sometimes staff tend to use the extreme nature of the special needs of children to justify lack of access to certain curriculum areas or school facilities, instead of searching for ways of opening access to all children. It is worth looking at the ways other schools group children in order to assess the most appropriate model for an individual school. The original reason for establishing a particular system may not be valid on close inspection, since children grow, change and develop and staff gain in skills.

The nature of a child's behaviour problems will of necessity influence decisions of access to the community. All children should be able to use the community resources as fully as possible, but, in the case of young people who display serious violent or aggressive outbursts or extremely anti-social behaviour, places to visit need to be selected with care. Consideration must be given not only to the safety of the child in this circumstance, but also to the safety of parents, staff and members of the public.

KEY POINTS

- All children have a right of access to all school facilities.
- Every effort needs to be made to open that access for the most disturbed child.

- Segregated provision can lead to under-expectation and in turn under-achievement.

- Attention needs to be paid to safety in relation to movement of some children throughout the community.

5 Breaks and lunchtimes

The question of supervision during *lunch and break times* was raised by the Elton Committee, who recognised the difficulties of supervisors and senior school staff who are responsible for the children. Break time is very stressful for staff and causes numerous upsets for children. The removal of structured support for children with behaviour problems increases pressure on them to control their behaviour with less support.

It is interesting to note how many children get into trouble during playtime and as a result are unsettled throughout the rest of the day. Many children with behaviour difficulties are noted by their inability to make positive friendships and to play appropriately. Children will not learn more appropriate patterns of behaviour by constantly being told off and by having all the class-based supports withdrawn from them. By using the building positively for some children or for small groups of children during these times, some problems can be minimised or avoided.

The change in staff during lunch breaks from teachers to lunchtime supervisors creates an additional series of problems in terms of management. Because there are fewer adults on duty and the children are usually in an unstructured setting, there are more opportunities for behaviour problems to occur. It is interesting to note what happens when children are expected to spend the whole of the lunch break outside – they make every effort to get inside; when expected to stay inside many children try to abscond. A way round this is to 'allow' children to choose by planning activities in certain areas of the school that are open to children during the break. This is particularly appropriate for secondary pupils who may consider it more grown-up to listen to music, play cards, work in independent learning bases or read a book. If the school rules are clearly upheld in this as in all other situations, the emphasis will be upon respect for others and their property and being courteous and considerate. Youngsters who display extreme behaviour difficulties would need support to choose and, probably, close supervision to manage this situation. If their difficulties were severe, they would be having close supervision and support anyway.

In certain situations classes may be timetabled for outside play. This serves a useful purpose for many children with behaviour problems because the unstructured and often disorganised opportunity for 'free play' afforded by the normal mid-morning or midday playtimes can result in a marked deterioration in behaviour. The transfer from an organised and carefully planned teaching situation to a free-for-all is often too much for children to cope with. There is a view that all children need to let off steam, but it should not be at the expense of a child's overall progress and positively fostered relationships with other children. Careful grading of free playtime will be beneficial as the child learns to cope with, first, the changes in expectation and, second, the freedom to control his own behaviour.

Flexibility in the use of dining facilities within schools is not always possible, but established practice needs to be challenged from time to time. It is usually considered appropriate for children to eat together in a central hall or dining-room, as long as they can cope with the additional noise and movement. It is difficult to supervise large groups of children in the dining-room, as it is in the playground, and problems can arise that could have been avoided in the smaller class situation. A group of children eating in the classroom has a more settled environment, where structured programmes can be followed successfully; and their moving from the main dining area decreases noise and creates space for more flexibile grouping. Some classes would benefit from staying in their own classroom during breaks, if there were staff to supervise them. As with all other decisions, attention would need to be given to the selection of the group and the reasons why that group had been chosen would have to be shared; for example, the leavers group might benefit from a more adult-orientated lunchtime in a different area of the school, creating the same effect in the main dining-room as removing the nursery class.

It is important to provide some form of training for lunchtime supervisors in the care and management of children in the playground and during mealtimes. Many problems can be avoided by an increased understanding of unnecessary confrontation, not arguing with children, use of voice, and close attention to supervision. One of the biggest difficulties here is the limited time that the lunchtime supervisors are available for work, which limits opportunities for training. The involvement of the Head or deputy in the playground or around the school during break periods gives a unique opportunity for training by example. The five minutes after duty when the dinner supervisors have their cup of tea before going home provides plenty of opportunities to talk through some of the issues that occurred during the break. On most occasions, staff are keen to share their concerns (and successes) and value the opportunity to talk through what has happened.

KEY POINTS

- Break periods are potentially one of the most difficult times during the day for children with additional behaviour problems.

- Changes and reductions in staff result in lack of consistency and the withdrawal of necessary support for the children.

- Training for dinner supervisors is very important, even if it is only through frequent, short opportunities for discussion.

- School buildings and facilities need to be used flexibly during break times.

6 Safety issues in relation to the building

It is important for all staff and pupils to know which areas are potentially dangerous either for children or for children and staff. Clear rules on *'out of bounds'* areas need to be established and all children and staff need to be aware of them. The school health and safety programme should include the reasons for such decisions for those children who are able to understand about taking unnecessary risks and danger. For example, kitchen areas in most schools are out of bounds if they are used to cater for large groups of people; laundry facilities may have industrial machines; workshops should be used only when children are accompanied by a member of staff. Such rules, once established, must be enforced for the safety of staff and children alike. Young people who are deliberately defiant in the face of rules may need to be protected by doors being locked. Those children who do not understand the need for certain rules will have to be closely supervised to ensure their safety.

A school which opens straight on to a main road, and which caters for children who run indiscriminately, would have no choice but to keep the front door locked when children are on the premises as a preventive measure. The locked door does not teach children why it is dangerous to run straight out of a building, but that lesson can be taught during a structured programme planned to meet the individual needs of the child himself, when staff or parents can supervise closely. Keys would need to be made available to staff, or an easy unlocking device to ensure that children and adults could evacuate the building safely in case of fire. In classrooms, furniture may be used to prevent a child running indiscriminately from a room; it is often enough to use the furniture to give the adult time to catch the child rather than to barricade the class into the room (see chapter 3).

Store cupboards containing dangerous or poisonous substances must of course be kept locked. This would include cleaning materials as well as dangerous equipment and might also include electrical equipment. Some children find it tempting to plug equipment into sockets without sufficient awareness of danger to avoid using, for example, wet plugs. Children may be tempted by disinfectant and other coloured liquids that remind them of soft drinks. The safe storage of poisonous and dangerous substances does not, of course, apply only to children with additional behaviour problems; all children need to be protected by careful storage.

The use of tools in the CDT room and gardening implements will need close supervision and probably their own safety rules. It may be that children with severe problems cannot use such equipment without one-to-one supervision; equipment should never be left around without supervision.

These are merely a few examples of the range of health and safety considerations that would apply in any school, with any children. When children cannot see potential danger and hazards, the safety regulations will need to be adhered to all the more stringently.

KEY POINTS

- It is vital for a detailed checklist on all the above issues to be held by every member of staff.

- As we have seen, many aspects of organisation can affect the school's ability to support children with behaviour problems. Attention to the use of resources, be they human, physical or environmental, will help the staff in identifying areas where change will lead to more successful and less stressful management of children.

6
Establish the framework

Having covered such a wide range of issues within the previous chapters it is important to end up by ensuring that some straightforward guidelines are provided at the end of the book to ensure that an esential framework could be established to support children with behaviour problems in any school. Provided that a sound base is established, many of the procedures which have been discussed can be steadily introduced.

The framework will answer the following questions:

- Can a statement be made on the areas which will make the school a caring school?
- Leadership is crucial. What can realistically be expected from the Head teacher?
- What leadership can be expected from a head of department or class teacher?
- What are the essential systems that need to be in place in a school to ensure that children with behaviour problems do not fall through the net?

1 Clarity of expectation

Whatever the type of school, and whatever the severity of the learning difficulty or behaviour problem, it is vital for a school to establish and share a 'mission statement' in regard to expectation of behaviour. It goes without saying that any such statement should be regularly reviewed, and also that all those involved with the school will need to be regularly reminded of it. Many people will consider this statement to provide the ethos of the school, but it must be a sharp, easily definable tool established out of consultation and negotiation.

Whilst such a statement is clearly an internal school document it is vital that it be established with the awareness and support of the community in which the school is based.

The diagram below provides an indication of many of the areas which

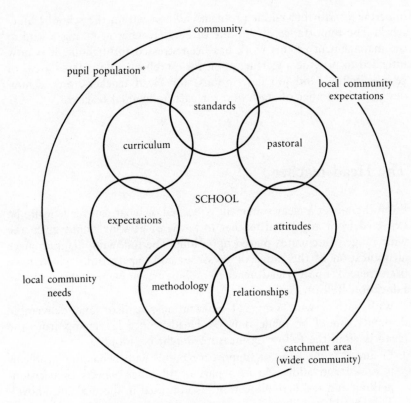

community

pupil population*

local community
expectations

standards

curriculum

pastoral

SCHOOL

expectations

attitudes

local community
needs

methodology

relationships

catchment area
(wider community)

* boys and girls/ethnic minorities/disabilities

may be included in such a statement. The following two areas can be used as examples:

Relationships   It is important for a school to make an explicit statement of its expectations with regard to relationships – between peers; different age groups; pupils and staff at different year groups; pupils and parents; pupils and adults within the community.

Methodology   It follows that there needs to be a statement on how the teaching styles and teaching/learning relationships will be established within a school to establish those relationships and provide each individual with a sense of value and independence.

2 *Establishing clear leadership*

It has been stated throughout the book that it is vital for the Head teacher to take a clear lead in establishing the importance of work undertaken with behaviour problem children within the school framework. The importance of the role of every teacher in taking a lead in the management of this work has been stressed throughout. It is now intended to provide a starting point for establishing designated areas of responsibility, (and job descriptions) for Head teachers, any 'senior' designated member of staff, and for each individual teacher.

The Head teacher

From the outset a clear statement is needed of what can realistically be expected from any Head teacher in terms of personal input given the wide range of demands placed upon him. The following diagram gives an indication of the range of pressures and expectations which have been placed upon Head teachers following implementation of the Education Reform Act.

With such a wide range of expectations, realistic and deliverable demands should be made only on Heads. Since leadership from the Head is vital, the following measures might be adopted.

1 Ensure that the issue of support for pupils with behaviour problems is raised and addressed as a part of all other aspects of decision-making and resource allocation (as indicated in the diagram above). This should steadily raise awareness and gain a commitment to work in this area from all staff.

2 Establish a management structure within the staff to support work in this area (whether within pastoral, curriculum, senior management or special staff areas).

3 Establish a clear system of responsibility/accountability within the school for handling individual issues. Such a system should involve *all* teachers having individual responsibility.

4 Ensure that there are effective communication systems in this area within the school.

5 Ensure that there are effective communication systems in this area between the school and parents, governors and the community.

6 Establish a system for monitoring and evaluating work done in this area, especially decision-making by staff, consistency of work records, sanctions, etc.

7 Ensure that some priority is given to INSET in this area.

8 Ensure that the handling of pupils' behaviour is built into any staff appraisal scheme in a supportive manner.

9 Be aware, and willing, on occasion to support staff and pupils by managing particular pupils when specific problems occur.

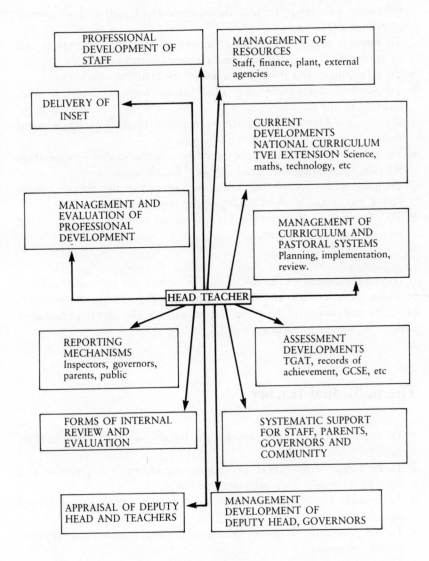

The senior 'designated' member of staff

It is quite likely, and very appropriate, for a Head teacher to ask one senior member of staff to take a specific lead role in the development of behavioural support within the school. In small or special schools this may be a deputy head or senior teacher, in large schools it may be the group of pastoral or faculty heads. The following shows the range of responsibilities held by such a post holder:

1 To establish a whole-school system for the support of pupils with

behaviour problems. To include all member of staff and all aspects of review procedures.

2 To monitor and evaluate the effectiveness of work undertaken and to report on it to the Head teacher, parents and governors.

3 To co-ordinate and manage the in-service training of all staff.

4 To support assessment and observation work undertaken with individual pupils.

5 To act as a first line of advice to members of staff on behavioural issues.

6 To link with specialist support staff outside the school – inspectors, advisers, psychologists, social services, health workers, etc.

7 To liaise with parents and community groups in the area to ensure better access and understanding of the work done.

8 To co-ordinate all proposals for additional funding and resourcing for the work undertaken.

The establishment of the role (modified to suit the individual school) provides an immediate and direct support mechanism for all members of staff, and acknowledges the importance of the work undertaken within the school hierarchy.

The individual teacher

1 To accept direct responsibility for the behaviour of all pupils in their care.

2 To be aware of the school procedures for identification, review and support of pupils with behaviour problems.

3 To provide a consistent response to all pupils within agreed school guidelines.

4 To keep records of pupil behavioural development and monitor pupils' progress.

5 To provide a secure, caring, controlled environment for pupils.

6 To establish relationships with pupils, so that they feel able to relate, and to provide counselling.

7 When necessary, to assess the particular needs of pupils and develop a support programme with the help and guidance of the designated member of staff.

8 To receive minutes of review meetings on individual pupils and support a whole school behavioural programme when in contact with those pupils.

3 *What essential systems are needed?*

To develop appropriate support for pupils with behaviour problems every school will need three basic systems for collecting information, establishing priorities and making decisions. The following examples can be adapted as necessary to meet the needs of an individual school.

Gathering information

At the outset of any scheme, it is important to gather a broad and accurate baseline of information on which to build. It becomes virtually a 'stock-take' of all issues which are relevant to the development of a particular issue. The example provided comes from the draft Birmingham LEA document, which incorporated aspects of behavioural support into the pastoral care area. This schedule of review was developed between advisers and Head teachers from primary, secondary and special schools, working together in a joint approach.

Pastoral care

Aims and objectives

1 How is the school's policy on pastoral care implemented, monitored and reviewed?
2 How is the policy shared with parents?
3 How are the aims and objectives reflected in the school's working practice?

Structure, organisation and management
1 What is the staffing structure for pastoral care and does it take account of the need to maintain a record of achievement scheme?
2 What is the support system for both pupils and staff?
3 How is the importance of pastoral care represented within the school as a whole and within the curriculum in particular?
4 What provision is made for regular meetings between pastoral care staff?
5 What are the links between form tutors, pastoral leaders and senior staff, curriculum leaders and parents?
6 What system exists for teachers to draw upon the experience of other staff when they feel a pupil needs special care?
7 How does the pastoral system involve pupils in the management of change within the school?

---

8 How does the school meet the training needs of teaching and non-teaching staff with particular reference to personal education?

Relationships

1 What is the quality of interaction between pupils and teachers during collective activities, such as assemblies, lunches, movement around the school?
2 What is the quality of relationships and mutual regard between pupils and teachers in the classroom situation?
3 What evidence is there of mutual respect between pupils and teachers in the counselling situation?
4 What is the quality of interaction between pupils during collective activities and in the classroom situation?
5 How are parents enabled to feel welcomed and appropriately informed when coming into the school?
6 To what extent are parents increasingly involved as partners with teachers in the welfare and development of pupils?
7 What is the quality of interaction between all members of the staff?
8 To what extent are relationships between senior management and other staff open, with a free flow of information and with the opportunity for each to put their point of view?

Counselling, guidance and learning support

1 Are there members of staff who are recognised as having counselling and guidance skills?
2 To what extent are pupils able, with ease, to seek out particular members of staff, who, they feel, can offer them the understanding, help or information they need?
3 What opportunities are there for group counselling?
4 Is there a comfortable space designated for private counselling?
5 What points of personal contact are available to every student and every parent?
6 How is the confidentiality of information maintained between counsellor and counselled?
7 What links are there with supporting agencies beyond the school?

Rewards, sanctions and responsibilities

1 What evidence is there that the ethos of the school reflects a positive recognition of pupils' achievements and qualities?
2 How are pupils encouraged to value and celebrate successes of all kinds and to learn positively from other experiences?

3 To what extent are there corporate decisions, which include pupils, about school sanctions?
4 What support is offered to staff, pupils and their parents to establish and maintain good working relationships?
5 How are pupils encouraged to view the responsibilities they take on as an integral part of the corporate life of the school?

Consistency of experience, progression
1 What system exists to ensure that pupils experience balanced and consistent pastoral support throughout their school career?
2 What provision is there for regular liaison between pastoral care staff and subject departmental heads/post holders with special responsibilities?
3 What provision is there to ensure the involvement of ancillary staff in the delivery of the pastoral aims of the school?
4 What monitoring system exists within the pastoral structure to ensure appropriate reaction to a pupil's progress or regression?
5 What system exists to ensure effective liaison with feeder schools and post-school provision?

Links with external agencies
1 How is the responsibility for liaising with external agencies managed by the school?
2 What professional support do these external agencies provide to the school's pastoral function?
3 What training and staff development exists for form tutors to improve liaison with home, the community and external agencies?

Establishing priorities and decision making

It is vital before establishing any programme/scheme to ensure that you really are planning and committing resources to a scheme that is appropriate. Any development needs the commitment of staff and must, therefore, be established with their involvement. It is important, especially in the area of behaviour problems, that staff are aware of the system being used to establish priorities and make decisions so that they may contribute and feel that they have been involved in decision making. Such simple systems will also prove invaluable to governors, when they can easily understand their role in the decision-making procedure.

When working with pupils with behaviour problems it often becomes difficult to stand back and put all that is going on into perspective without feeling threatened or under stress. It has to be remembered, however, that both adults and pupils share the same needs, and the

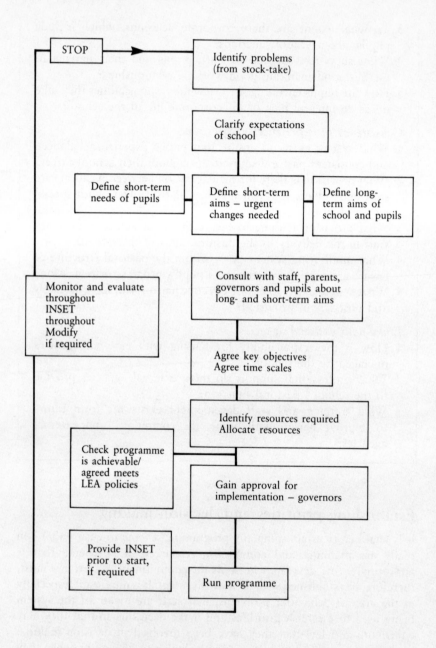

system and procedures offered in this book attempt to ensure that these needs are met. Both groups have a need for responsibility, a need to live and work in a system which enables constant self-discipline rather than imposing external discipline, and both groups hope for an enhanced self-image which develops in response to effort and praise. For quality of life both groups need to be able to grow within a warm and caring environment.

Good Luck.

Further reading

Chisholm, B., et al (1986) *Preventive approaches to disruption (PAD)*, Macmillan Educational.

Birmingham Education Authority (1989) Draft Paper on School Review.

Docking, J.W. (1980) *Control and Discipline in Schools*, Harper and Row.

Elton et al (1989) *Discipline in Schools – Report of the Committee of Enquiry* Chaired by Lord Elton, HMSO.

Fish, J. (1985) *Educational Opportunities for All*, ILEA.

Foxen, T. and McBrian, J. (1981) *Training Staff in Behavioural Methods* (Trainee Workbook), Manchester University Press.

Galloway, D., et al (1982) *Schools and Disruptive Pupils*, Longman.

Gray, J. and Richer, J. (1988) *Classroom Responses to Disruptive Behaviour*, Macmillan Educational.

Hargreaves, D.H. (1984) *Improving Secondary Schools*, ILEA.

Herbert, M. (1981) *Behavioural Treatment of Problem Children*, Academic Press.

Kiernan, C. and Jones, M. (1982) *Behaviour Assessment Battery*, NFER.

Kyriacou, C. (1986) *Effective Teaching in Schools*, Basil Blac..well.

Leach, D.J. and Raybould, E.C. (1977) *Learning and Behaviour Difficulties in School*, Open Books.

Mager, R.F. (1974) *Goal Analysis*, Fearon Publishers.

Murphy, G. and Wilson, B. (1985) *Self Injurious Behaviour*, British Institute of Mental Handicaps.

Reid, A.H. (1982) *The Psychiatry of Mental Handicap*, Blackwell Scientific.

Robertson, J. (1981) *Effective Classroom Control*, Hodder and Stoughton.

Topping, K.J. (1983) *Educational Systems for Disruptive Adolescents*, Croom Helm.

Westmacott, E.W. and Cameron, E.J. (1981) *Behaviour Can Change*, Globe Educational.

Wheldell, K. and Merrett, F. (1985) *Manual for the Behavioural Approach to Teaching Package (BATpack)*, Positive Products.

Wragg, E.C. (ed) (1984) *Classroom Teaching Skills*, Croom Helm.

Key points index

To enable readers to identify major issues and therefore easily find support.

Notes

Notes

Notes